Currencies, Capital Flows and Crises

Breaking from conventional wisdom, this book provides an explanation of exchange rates based on the premise that it is financial capital flows and not international trade that represents the driving force behind currency movements. John T. Harvey combines analyses rooted in the scholarly traditions of John Maynard Keynes and Thorstein Veblen with that of modern psychology to produce a set of new theories to explain international monetary economics, including not only exchange rates but also world financial crises.

In the book, the traditional approach is reviewed and critiqued and the alternative is then built by studying the psychology of the market and balance-of-payments questions. The central model has at its core Keynes' analysis of the macroeconomy and it assumes neither full employment nor balanced trade over the short or long run. Market participants' mental model, which they use to forecast future exchange rate movements, is specified and integrated into the explanation. A separate but related discussion of currency crises shows that three distinct tension points emerge in booming economies, any one of which can break and signal the collapse. Each of the models is compared to post-Bretton Woods history and the reader is shown exactly how various shifts and adjustments on the graphs can explain the dollar's ups and downs and the Mexican (1994) and Asian (1997) crises.

Post Keynesians, Institutionalists, and other heterodox economists will find much to admire in this volume, as will students and researchers engaged with exchange rate determination, international capital flows, and international financial crises.

John T. Harvey is Professor of Economics at Texas Christian University.

Routledge Advances in Heterodox Economics
Edited by Frederic S. Lee
University of Missouri-Kansas City

Over the past two decades, the intellectual agendas of heterodox economists have taken a decidedly pluralist turn. Leading thinkers have begun to move beyond the established paradigms of Austrian, feminist, Institutional-evolutionary, Marxian, Post Keynesian, radical, social, and Sraffian economics – opening up new lines of analysis, criticism, and dialogue among dissenting schools of thought. This cross-fertilization of ideas is creating a new generation of scholarship in which novel combinations of heterodox ideas are being brought to bear on important contemporary and historical problems.

Routledge Advances in Heterodox Economics aims to promote this new scholarship by publishing innovative books in heterodox economic theory, policy, philosophy, intellectual history, institutional history, and pedagogy. Syntheses or critical engagement of two or more heterodox traditions are especially encouraged.

1 **Ontology and Economics**
Tony Lawson and his critics
Edited by Edward Fullbrook

2 **Currencies, Capital Flows and Crises**
A Post Keynesian analysis of exchange rate determination
John T. Harvey

This series was previously published by The University of Michigan Press and the following books are available (please contact UMP for more information):

Economics in Real Time
A theoretical reconstruction
John McDermott

Liberating Economics
Feminist perspectives on families, work, and globalization
Drucilla K. Barker and Susan F. Feiner

Socialism After Hayek
Theodore A. Burczak

Future Directions for Heterodox Economics
Edited by John T. Harvey and Robert F. Garnett, Jr.

Currencies, Capital Flows and Crises

A Post Keynesian analysis of exchange rate determination

John T. Harvey

Routledge
Taylor & Francis Group

LONDON AND NEW YORK

Transferred to digital printing 2010

First published 2009
by Routledge
2 Park Square, Milton Park, Abingdon, Oxon, OX14 4RN

Simultaneously published in the USA and Canada
by Routledge
270 Madison Avenue, New York, NY 10016

Routledge is an imprint of the Taylor & Francis Group, an informa business

© 2009 John T. Harvey
Typeset in Times New Roman by Pindar NZ, Auckland, New Zealand

British Library Cataloguing in Publication Data
A catalogue record for this book is available from the British Library

Library of Congress Cataloging-in-Publication Data
Harvey, John T., 1961-
  Currencies, capital flows, and crises : a post Keynesian analysis of
exchange rate determination / John T. Harvey.
    p. cm.
  Includes bibliographical references and index.
  ISBN 978-0-415-77763-6 (hb)—ISBN 978-0-203-88478-2 (eb)
  1. Foreign exchange rates. 2. Capital movements. 3. Currency. I. Title.
  HG3851.H376 2008
  332.4'56—dc22   2008027278

ISBN10: 0-415-77763-1 (hbk)
ISBN10: 0-415-78120-5 (pbk)
ISBN10: 0-203-88478-7 (ebk)

ISBN13: 978-0-415-77763-6 (hbk)
ISBN13: 978-0-415-78120-6 (pbk)
ISBN13: 978-0-203-88478-2 (ebk)

Contents

Figures

Acknowledgments

This book has taken almost two decades to come to fruition. From the year I left graduate school in 1987, I knew I wanted to study exchange rates; but, deciding what to add to the conversation took a very long time. I would not regard those intervening years as a struggle, however, as I thoroughly enjoyed every step. I owe the greatest thanks to my wife and twin daughters not only because they put up with the frequent interruptions in their lives, but especially because they shared my enthusiasm throughout this project. It is to them that I dedicate this volume.

Others I would like to thank are, first and foremost, my parents for their example and support (and, more recently, watching the kids!); the late Hans E. Jensen, my first undergraduate economics teacher at the University of Tennessee (and later a member of my dissertation committee), who not only inspired me to major in the field but has been my role model ever since; Paul Davidson, editor of the *Journal of Post Keynesian Economics*, for his considerable help and encouragement over the years; my principal at Knoxville Catholic High School, the Reverend Xavier Mankel, who made sure that I was taking full advantage of the opportunities available to me; and finally to my friends and colleagues Ilene Grabel and Julio Lopez, who have gone above and beyond in their helpful comments, criticism, and advice. Life is path dependent, and I have been fortunate to have the all the above influence me.

1 Introduction

From 1980 to 1985, the value of the dollar in terms of the Deutsche Mark more than doubled. Immediately thereafter (and in less time) it did a complete reversal. In December of 1994, the Mexican peso lost almost sixty percent of its value against the dollar in just two weeks. The South Korean won plummeted from 891 per dollar on August 4, 1997, to 1,812 by January 9 of the next year. At the time of this writing (spring 2008) the dollar is in the midst of a historic collapse. Each of these extraordinary upheavals was accompanied by macro consequences that went well beyond currency markets and shifted economic activity onto new paths. These were not trivial events or a sideshow, they were center stage.

Despite the central importance of the market for foreign currency, mainstream economists are unable to agree on how it works. There is no single, well-accepted explanation (as in neoclassical trade theory, for example), but a smorgasbord of choices. These include, though are not limited to, purchasing power parity, the monetary model, the Dornbusch model, portfolio balance, Mundell-Fleming, currency substitution, fundamentalists versus chartists, microstructure studies, and order flow. While there is some agreement on the general principles that 1) short-run movements may be driven by non-fundamental factors (some going so far as to admit that less-than-rational expectations may play a role) and 2) long-run currency prices move economies toward optimal levels (typically a balanced-trade equilibrium), there appears to be little interest in modeling the former and little agreement on the specifics of the latter.

The simultaneous co-existence of so many approaches along with a general shift to long-run studies is a function of the poor empirical performance of each individual Neoclassical model. First highlighted by Richard Meese and Kenneth Rogoff (1983), these troubles have continued unabated (Rogoff 2001), so much so that it is now common to include a mention of this even at the textbook level.[1] The real problem, of course, is the fact that the Neoclassical paradigm is poorly equipped to explain a world marked by less-than-full employment, fundamental uncertainty, endogenous money, historical time, equilibrium trade imbalances, and agents whose preferences and worldviews are a function of social rather than internal and atomistic influences. This is glaringly obvious over the short run, though no less true in the long run.

By contrast, the model developed in this book has no difficulty in explaining modern currency markets. Coming from the Post Keynesian perspective, it resorts to neither "ad hocery" nor special cases to account for the salient features of the international financial system and it is a single, coherent explanation. The unique element of the approach adopted here is the assumption that portfolio capital flows are not, in either the short or long run, passive and accommodating, but an independent and dominant force in setting exchange rates. In such a world, subjective speculative pressures can create wild swings in prices and, unless agents happen by coincidence to focus on trade balances as the primary factor driving their forecast of future exchange rate movements, there is no reason to believe that international flows of goods and services play any more than a secondary role in determining currency prices over any time horizon. Furthermore and in contrast to the mainstream practice, agents' expectations are modeled as a real, causal element in the determination of currency prices and not simply as the source of white noise around a long-term, fundamental trend. This is a strong break and will require forays into Institutionalism and psychology, as well as Post Keynesian economics.

What evidence is there to justify shifting the focus (short and long term) to capital flows? That their absolute volume is extremely large is undeniable. A 2004 *Bank for International Settlements* (BIS) survey of currency markets showed that the average daily value of currency transactions (based on April of that year and net of double counting) was around $1.9 trillion (BIS 2005: 1) – enough to accommodate world trade 40 times over (BIS 2005: 1; *World Trade Organization* 2005: 3). Even assuming a number of covering transactions for each import and export, it is clear that the overwhelming majority of foreign exchange transactions are related to capital. Mainstream economics does not necessarily deny this, but assumes that these activities have no net long-run impact on currency prices. Either they are white noise or they are a mere reflection of trade flows.

Whether or not this last point is true is crucial. If it is the case that capital flows have no lasting effect on foreign exchange prices then, for all intents and purposes, currency demand arises only from import-export transactions. In that event, short-term trade imbalances would indeed be as fleeting as argued in mainstream economics. Consider that argument. When a nation imports, they supply their home money in exchange for foreign so that they can use the latter to buy foreign goods and services. Imports thus translate into home currency supply. When they export, this creates a demand for their currency as foreigners buy it to obtain the home country's goods and services: exports are home currency demand. Therefore, any country with a trade deficit must necessarily be experiencing an excess supply of the home currency, driving its price lower and making their products increasingly inexpensive. This process continues until balanced trade is restored. Meanwhile, countries with trade surpluses would be witness to own-currency appreciation until balance was restored.

So, in a world where capital flows are white noise or a reflection of trade flows, current accounts would tend toward balance. Exchange rate models would logically focus on imports and exports as the primary determinants of currency prices, particularly over the long run. In addition, because trade flows change only slowly, the international monetary system would be marked by smoothly adjusting currency prices. In a world where trade flows rule the roost, volatility and trade imbalances would be the exception. Capital flows may add some short-term drama, but they would have no lasting effect.

Now imagine instead if the factors driving those massive financial capital flows were fundamentally distinct from those determining trade flows, undertaken by different people with different agendas, worldviews, goals, et cetera. In that event, just because a nation is experiencing a trade imbalance does not mean that its currency price is out of line with its short- or long-term equilibrium. Recall that in the example in the previous paragraph the nation in question experienced a currency price depreciation because the trade deficit was evidence of an excess supply of its currency. But with large and independent capital flows, the trade balance tells only a small part of the story. So long as the nation in question is running a capital account surplus to offset the trade deficit, it is quite possible that their currency price is stable and could even be appreciating, just as the US dollar was during the rising trade deficits of the early 1980s. The tendency towards balanced trade is gone.[2] In addition, because the pursuit of short-term capital gain is driven by subjective and potentially unstable factors, the magnitude and direction of capital flows can change very quickly. Bandwagon effects, over-reaction, and fluctuating levels of confidence in agents' forecasts combine to create a very different market dynamic than that created by trade flows. This is the world described by the models in this book and, more importantly, it is the one in which we live.

INSTITUTIONALIST AND POST KEYNESIAN ECONOMICS AND PSYCHOLOGY

Institutionalist economics

Though the Post Keynesian influence on this volume is the most obvious, the analysis is firmly and self-consciously set in an Institutionalist framework. Institutionalists view the economy from a broad perspective wherein markets are perceived as social institutions

> like democracy and marriage ... not physical phenomena such as light waves or friction. They serve to organize and guide human behavior through sanctions (formal and informal, negative and positive), mores, norms, status, and shared worldviews. Activities of markets are the activities of people and societies.
> (Harvey 1993b: 679)

Capitalism (or any form of economic organization) is no more "natural" than the English language, indentured servitude, or Major League Baseball. Each is the result of a particular line of social evolution. In contrast to mainstream suggestions that economic behavior is subject to immutable laws, Institutionalism asserts that we are not dealing with universal phenomena. While there certainly are generalities (as explained below), they are to be discovered and not assumed.

Social institutions recreate themselves through constant evaluation of the behavior of their members. Behavior that meets the social standard is rewarded and thus encouraged and perpetuated; that which does not is punished. Because humans are social animals, this is done primarily by the members themselves as they strive to adhere to established conventions and thereby gain the approval of the "tribe" (the other members of the gang, fellow Texans, or the subculture of currency dealers, for example).[3] According to Institutionalists, the relevant evaluative criteria can be divided into two sets: instrumental and ceremonial. Acts sanctioned by the former are rational and pragmatic. Something is "right" because it works, without reference to the way things were done before. Instrumental values lead to goal-oriented, experimental, and progressive action and they contribute to social provisioning (providing for the basic needs of all members of the economy) and democratic problem-solving (resolving the issues faced by the average person). By contrast, ceremony is concerned with tradition and power. A pattern of behavior is justified by appeal to the past and often implies invidious distinction. The tradition in western culture that a woman takes the surname of her husband, for example, is defended simply on the basis of "that is the way it is done" and it is, at least historically, an indication of her status as de facto property.

Societies and subcultures dominated by ceremonial valuing are marked by institutions that tend to be exploitative rather than creative. One manifestation of this occurs when groups and individuals focus on devising means of keeping or taking power, goods, wealth, land, et cetera from others not identified by some culture-specific standard as "us." This is very common in nations with serious ethnic, religious, political, or other divisions and is a frequent problem in developing nations. Developed economies are not immune, however, and the nature and effect of institutions like sexism and racism can be explained by ceremony. Institutionalists also describe "business" as a ceremonial phenomenon. The goal of business is the accumulation of wealth and hence its orientation is power and exploitation, not democratic problem-solving. If policy makers can create an environment in which businesses only achieve wealth if they have solved some social problem, then it is possible to link the ceremonial to the instrumental. But in general it is important to remember that encouraging business is not equivalent to encouraging social welfare.[4]

What all this means for foreign exchange is that, first, a key consideration must be to determine the manner in which the institution is organized and whether this organization is conducive to social provisioning or exploitation. This theme runs throughout this book, if often in the background, and therefore the analysis must delve into the specific subculture of currency markets as well as the worldviews of those therein. It also means there is no a priori assumption that markets are the best way to solve social problems or that they are inherently flawed or morally wrong. Markets are tools, no more and no less; their propriety is a function of their ability to solve the problem at hand. Nor is it assumed that market behavior is rational (by whatever definition). Markets are people in a particular social setting. What markets reflect, reward, and encourage is a direct function of what is reflected, rewarded, and encouraged in that society. If a culture is racist, an employer daring to hire a member of the oppressed race may lose sales as customers turn away. If in an asset market agents focus on sun spots in forecasting future prices, those not doing so will find themselves with depreciating portfolios. That markets are people and people are social animals is an important premise of this work and the primary influence of the Institutionalist approach on this volume.

Post Keynesian economics

While the Institutionalist perspective is vital in understanding the context in which the market for foreign exchange exists and the manner in which it is organized, this book can best be described as Post Keynesian. The latter is indispensable in this endeavor because it offers unique insight into the working of modern capitalist economies and into the primary factor driving foreign currency prices: asset markets. Post Keynesians trace their intellectual heritage to John Maynard Keynes. Like Keynes, they see the assumption that agents view the future to be uncertain as critical to understanding real world economies. It is because of this that economies can come to rest at less-than-full employment. This is best explained through an example.

Assume a closed economy with no government sector. Let Y represent aggregate output, income, and expenditure (each of which must be equal to the other in a closed system), S aggregate savings, C aggregate consumption, and I aggregate investment.[5] There are only two sectors: households and firms; and for simplicity let only the former earn income, consume, and save while only the latter may borrow (which, since they do not retain earnings, they must do in order to invest).

Household income (Y) can be either spent (as consumption, or C) or saved (S). This is shown in 1.1:

$$Y = C + S \qquad\qquad 1.1$$

Equation 1.2 illustrates the fact that since there are only two types of goods in the macro-economy, total expenditures (also Y) can only have been on consumption(C) or investment (I):

$$Y = C + I \qquad\qquad 1.2$$

Equation 1.2 can also be derived from the fact that all output produced (Y) must either be in the form of consumption goods (C) or investment goods (I).

The clear implication of 1.1 and 1.2 is S = I. In other words, in equilibrium, total savings must equal total investment. That this is true under the assumptions made above is not a point of contention within either the mainstream or Post Keynesian schools of thought. Where they differ is in terms of the process by which the economy adjusts so that S and I come to rest at the same point and it is here that the role of uncertainty will become evident.

In the mainstream, interest rates bear the burden of adjustment. The key is that agents are assumed to know the future with at least probabilistic certainty.[6] This has important consequences. For example, in the absence of concern about unforeseen events agents have little desire to save. Their demand for goods and services is insatiable and so they will spend all current income if they are not somehow rewarded for doing otherwise.

But they are so rewarded with interest. When financial institutions offer higher interest, households save more; when they offer lower interest, households save less. Interest is thus the compensation for not consuming. Note that this implies that households never save cash. Rather, all savings would be held (assuming, for simplicity, a choice between cash and bonds) in the form of interest-bearing bonds, the proceeds from the sale of which can then be loaned out by the issuer (to firms, who need to borrow in order to invest). To summarize, households only save because they are offered interest, all savings are held in bonds, and the proceeds from bond sales are available to firms wishing to borrow to invest.

Now imagine this economy at full-employment equilibrium with S = I. Say that, for whatever reason, firms decide to invest less. This temporarily leaves us at S > I and with the threat of economic contraction. But given that S, because it is held in bonds, is equivalent to the stock of loanable funds and since I is the sole source of borrowing, S > I also means that financial institutions have excess balances. Since they pay interest on deposits and only earn income if those funds are loaned out, this creates an incentive to lower the interest rate (to both discourage deposits and encourage borrowers). As this occurs, S (deposits) will fall and I (borrowing) will rise, both of which raise spending (since the fall in S means a rise in C) and help stave off the recession. This continues until S = I. In short, whenever S > I and recession looms, *interest rates automatically fall to reinvigorate spending* in the form of rising consumption and investment. Thus, in a world where the future is known, the financial sector responds directly to the needs of the real sector and there is never an obstacle to reaching full employment. Finance, money, portfolio capital, and all other monetary factors are irrelevant. It is the "real" side of the economy (those factors associated with output and employment) that rules the roost. In thinking about exchange rates, the implication of the Neoclassical approach is that our focus should be on trade flows rather than portfolio capital. The latter, regardless of its absolute size, is epiphenomenal; it is a result but not a cause.[7]

In Keynes' (and Post Keynesian) analysis, the fact of uncertainty changes the mechanism by which interest rates are determined and breaks the link described above. While it is still true that S will come to rest at the same level as I, the financial sector does not step in to solve the problem to everyone's benefit. Instead, the overall level of economic activity (Y) adjusts, sometimes causing expansion and sometimes recession. There exists no long- or short-run tendency to full employment.

In a world where the future is unknown, agents' insatiable demand is for wealth (goods, services, and assets) and not just goods and services. When one does not know what the future may bring, a stockpile of purchasing power for future eventualities will be forthcoming even without there being a reward for not consuming. As incomes rise, so households set aside more savings (and vice versa); but the volume of savings does not respond to interest rate movements. What interest does do is determine the manner in which savings are held. Agents face the tradeoff of holding cash, which is barren but provides quick and easy access to purchasing power (a priority if the future is unknown), or bonds, which yield interest but require time and possibly other transaction costs to liquidate. Interest is the reward for parting with the liquidity and safety offered by cash. Financial institutions offer higher interest not as a means of tempting agents to stop consuming and start saving, but to stop saving cash and start saving bonds. As the demand for liquidity rises (which it might do when agents become more concerned about the future and want to hoard cash or when they are eager to spend and temporarily hold money in anticipation of doing so), so interest rates rise as financial institutions must offer higher rates to attract buyers for bonds; as the demand falls, interest falls. Likewise, interest is inversely affected by the supply of liquidity, a supply that is partly exogenous (as governed by the central monetary authority) but largely endogenous. Discussing the latter will take us a little off track, so suffice it to say for now that Post Keynesians argue that money creation in modern capitalist economies is primarily private-market driven, rising and falling as financial institutions grant and destroy credit. In equilibrium, interest comes to rest at the point where the market for liquidity clears. Most important for the current discussion is the fact that S (savings) does not represent the stock of loanable funds; the latter is a multiple of the former because bank loans create money.

Returning to the scenario above, say that once again, having started in a position where S = I and full employment prevails, I falls. This time, there is no reason to expect an accommodating adjustment in the interest rate (which might in fact face upward pressure in light of the deteriorating conditions in the economy). Instead, the fall in investment induces recession. Workers are laid off, incomes fall, and, therefore, so does saving. Eventually, S = I once again, but at a lower level of Y and with less-than-full employment. Interest rates do not automatically fall as in the mainstream view, and even if they did they do not affect savings and have only a secondary effect on investment, the primary driver of which is the expectation of profit from investment. The financial sector is driven by a separate logic from the real economy. It might react in a manner that would help, with falling interest rates and easy access to liquidity, and it might hurt with rising interest rates and a liquidity squeeze. The bottom line, however, is that – unlike in the mainstream perception – it cannot be assumed that the financial sector quietly and obediently acts to solve problems arising in the real sector. In fact, the financial sector itself can be the source of problems. Changes there can have a long-run effect on output and employment. Back in the currency market, although trade flows (the real sector) can impact the currency price, the far larger and more volatile movements of short-term capital take center stage in today's economy. They are cause and not effect and we must understand them if we are to understand exchange-rate determination. This is an absolutely fundamental premise of the explanation of currency prices in this volume and is the most important component of the Post Keynesian contribution.

Post Keynesians also believe that history matters. This means that they believe the past has a real, qualitative impact on the future, that economic agents' decisions are affected by past events. As economic outcomes are realized, market participants' behavior adjusts and institutions evolve. This contrasts with the general equilibrium framework favored by the mainstream, within which everything happens simultaneously. That is, prices are set, contracts are struck, wages are earned, inputs are purchased, capital is built, incomes are spent, and output is produced all at the same instant (allowing for as much re-contracting as necessary, without cost, before the final agreements are struck). The economy reaches a state of equilibrium and stays there until one or more parameters change. The realized equilibrium does not somehow affect future ones by changing parameters (and therefore the underlying behavior). The parameters, the outcome, the equilibrium, and therefore the economy, are assumed stable in the general equilibrium approach.

With historical time, however, events evolve and emerge, and how they do so changes over time and is path dependent. Like the Austrians, Post Keynesians see the economy as a dynamic system rather than a static one. The short run is vitally important in the sense that it changes the possibilities for the long run. This is not to say that general equilibrium models are not appropriate or enlightening in some contexts. In general, however, it is important to bear in mind the dynamic nature of the economy and the limitations of modeling techniques that do not reflect this. This is why, when it comes to explaining agents' currency-price forecast determination in Chapter Five, the general equilibrium approach is abandoned in favor of a schematic. In addition, Post Keynesians do not expect their models to be deterministic predictors of the real world. Our analysis is a guide and it helps us create a common vocabulary and organize our thoughts. But the real world is too complex and changing to assume more than this. The evolution of history and institutions must be taken into account and they must be allowed to lead us to change our minds about how the economy works.

The Post Keynesian approach takes a different view of expectations than that found in Neoclassical economics. Because of their contention that financial markets play only a passive role, mainstream economists have never really seen the need for a sophisticated expectations-formation model for asset-market participants. In their view, what asset market participants expect is not a causal factor (Davidson 1982–83). The forecast and the object thereof are independent and thus the only question of concern is how accurate the prediction was (hence the role of rational expectations in the Neoclassical approach). But in the Post Keynesian world, the financial sector plays an important and independent role and agents' aggregate expectations drive the asset markets therein. Understanding how currency market participants decide that they should buy sterling rather than yen is absolutely vital.

Note that the fact that some mainstream models allow agents' expectations (and other financial factors) to play a causal role in the short run, but not the long run, is not seen by Post Keynesians as truly taking adequate account of their effect. This is because Post Keynesian economists see the long run as simply the accumulation of short runs. Drawing a distinction runs the risk of obscuring how crucial events in the short term have pushed the economy onto new paths or altered magnitudes or parameters in a significant and long-lasting manner. Short-run fluctuations are not only the most challenging to explain, they are the most important.

Psychology

The Institutionalist and Post Keynesian approaches suggest that it is important to develop a clear understanding of market participants' behavior. While Keynes provided insights in the *General Theory*, a clear picture cannot be had without reference to the work of psychologists Amos Tversky and Daniel Kahneman (1974). Their core argument is that in the real world people make decisions based on heuristics or rules of thumb. While these may sometimes lead to choices consistent with those that mainstream economists would expect (as guided by rational expectations and rational choice theory), there exist significant and not uncommon deviations and biases. These are not white noise. They are incorporated into the time series of the prices and shift economic activity onto new paths. In addition, they contribute to perceived patterns such as bandwagons, volatility, and profit taking. All of this is addressed in Chapter Three.

ORGANIZATION

Taking as it does elements of Institutionalist, Post Keynesian, and psychological theory, this book offers a unique perspective on the post-Bretton Woods currency market. Rather than ignoring or explaining away the massive rise in financial capital flows, it uses them as the central reason for volatile exchange rates that refuse to bow to central-bank pressure or respond to trade imbalances. Massive swings in currency prices are too common to be treated ad hoc. For those planning to use this book in the classroom, it is my hope that students will emerge with a much more realistic and useful conception of how the international monetary economy works.

This book is organized as follows. The next chapter, "Neoclassical approaches to exchange rate determination," reviews the most popular approaches to exchange rate determination. Special attention is paid to the manner in which capital flows are (or are not) modeled and the empirical performance of each theory. It will be shown that all Neoclassical models are based on the (implicit) assumption of continuous full employment, which then leads to the conclusion that only real factors (generally trade flows) drive the exchange rate. While some models allow for financial factors and expectations to have an impact in the short run, in the long run it is "real" variables that drive currency prices.

The next two chapters present the tools of analysis necessary for the construction of the Institutionalist/Post Keynesian approach. Chapter Three, "Psychology and decision-making in the foreign exchange market," takes the first step in creating an alternative exchange rate theory based on Institutionalist/Post Keynesian principles. One of the basic premises of this approach is that if portfolio capital flows dominate the market, and if portfolio capital flows are driven by agents' forecasts of future asset values, then any successful explanation of exchange rate movements must detail the manner in which market participants form expectations and make decisions. The chapter looks to the psychology literature for the basic building blocks of this view. In the process it is shown how social and psychological factors lead to bandwagons, cash in, price volatility, and the popularity of technical analysis. The concept of a mental model, or the theoretical understanding of the market that each agent uses to interpret events and predict the future, is also introduced in this chapter.

Chapter Four, "Leakages, injections, exchange rates and trade (im)balances," takes a short detour to show how exchange rates are related to balance of payments accounts. This is necessary because a central theme in Mainstream economics is that exchange rates tend to move in a way that causes countries to become equally competitive and net trade flows equal zero. Using a very basic graphical analysis, this chapter shows otherwise. The idea that there exists a "balance-trade exchange rate," or currency price at which balanced trade will prevail, is introduced here and then referenced in the next chapter.

Chapter Five is the heart of the book. Entitled "Post Keynesian exchange rate modeling," it develops two full-scale models. The goal of the first is to set the currency market inside a larger macroeconomy and show the interactions among the domestic macroeconomy, the financial market, trade and capital flows, and exchange rates. It is designed in such a way as to make it directly comparable to Mainstream approaches (a feature that is very helpful in the classroom). The product market is based on Keynes' aggregate supply-aggregate demand apparatus and the financial market is easily adapted to reflect money endogeneity and horizontalism versus verticalism. It assumes neither full employment nor balanced trade over any time horizon (although these states are possible).

While the first model allows changes in currency market participants' expectations to have real impact on economic variables, explaining how and why the former might change at all is left to the second. At its core is the mental model introduced in Chapter Three. This is agents' conception of the workings of currency market, which then generates their forecast of future movements of currency prices. This model is presented in a schematic format so that all variables and their interactions can be viewed at once. In addition, the key feedback loops in the market can be identified, particularly those associated with bandwagons, technical analysis, and the cash-in effect. The reader will be taken through a number of examples with each model. Interest rate parity is also discussed and a separate model to explain currency crises is presented. It includes factors from the mental model and incorporates Minsky's Financial Instability Hypothesis. Crises are seen as the inevitable consequence of agents' tendency to overreact to economic signals and to their proclivities for over-confidence and unfounded optimism.

Chapter Six, "Real-world applications," shows how foreign exchange markets since the collapse of Bretton Woods can be explained using the models developed in Chapter Five. Looking primarily at the dollar-Deutsche Mark/euro market, it does not simply suggest how one might use the models in understanding these events. Fresh graphs are drawn for every historical incident with each shift and flow illustrated. I hope that this is particularly useful to students since we so often leave them with little more than a hearty "good luck!" when it comes to showing how to apply the theories we have taught them. Also described in detail and in the context of the theory developed in Chapter Five are the Mexican and Asian financial crises.

Chapter Seven, "Problems and policy," reviews the various manners in which the international monetary system as currently designed frustrates our goals, and suggests policy to overcome these obstacles. The core conclusion of the book is that portfolio capital flows must be reduced and controlled. This will not be sufficient to solve all the world's problems, but it may make them more manageable. The market is **not** always right, and Keynes' admonition that "… the position is serious when enterprise becomes the bubble on a whirlpool of speculation" still applies today, perhaps more than ever (Keynes 1964: 159).[8]

Chapter Eight offers conclusions and thoughts on how Post Keynesians and Institutionalists can make their voices heard.

HOW TO USE THIS BOOK

Scholars

I have tried to make this book complete by supporting each element of my argument. However, many of those elements are already well known and accepted in Post Keynesian and Institutionalist economics. Hence, the experienced researcher might find such passages less interesting and may want to skip ahead. In that event, I would suggest starting with Chapter Five. Chapter Two is a critique of Neoclassical approaches and is therefore not essential to the central thesis, and Chapter Five begins with a quick review of what was covered in Chapters Three and Four. If questions arise, one can always return to earlier sections where necessary.

Students

Students were never far from my mind when I wrote this book. Not only did I hope to take what I learned from this experience and use it to help teach my courses, but in over twenty years of teaching I have always found students to be very open to the Post Keynesian approach. I believe this is because of its strong real-world focus. Students want to hear precisely how the financial system operates in a modern, industrial economy, not stories about helicopters. They instinctively share the Post Keynesian suspicion that the latter is not likely to be terribly helpful past the final exam date.

As a consequence, I hope that students buy this book and, particularly, that professors assign it in class. In Chapter Two I review the Neoclassical perspective, especially for instructors who feel an obligation to cover mainstream material (an obligation that I, too, felt until very recently). This way, you do not have to assign two books and the internet is an incredible source of any supplemental materials you may need. I also hope that the instructor schedules sufficient time to cover Chapter Six. It is there that the student will gain practice in using the model and they will, therefore, learn it properly and perhaps be able to take the lessons with them past graduation.

2 Neoclassical approaches to exchange rate determination[1]

The goal of this chapter is to offer a critical survey of those exchange rate theories put forward by the Neoclassical school of thought in economics. It will start with a review of the general characteristics of that school of thought, followed by a roughly chronological review of models from purchasing power parity to modern micro-based ones.

FOUNDATIONS OF NEOCLASSICAL ECONOMICS

Neoclassicism is diverse, so much so that one cannot easily create a list of universal traits. I will, therefore, limit my attention to those characteristics that are most commonplace and play an important role in their analyses of currency prices. To begin, understanding the Neoclassical approach to exchange rates requires an understanding of the fact that they view market systems as *natural*, at least in the sense that they are what humans would adopt if "external" influences did not force them to do otherwise. In addition, behavior therein is law governed. Markets, they argue, have existed throughout human history and have always been the preferred means of human economic interaction or, at the very least, the way humans would *rather* carry out production, distribution and allocation. As they are natural, their basic character does not vary over time or space. Hence, little by way of specific institutional or historical detail is necessary in order to construct reliable explanations of economic phenomena.

Also, economic agents are assumed to be the best judge of their own welfare and to be rational in the sense that they can consistently order these preferences and select the options that would maximize their welfare. Because markets allow these rational individuals the greatest freedom of choice, they are the most likely form of economic organization to generate outcomes that are beneficial to all parties. There are certainly exceptions to this, but even "market failure", the term applied to those situations, implies the primacy or default nature of market-based solutions. This tendency for an ex-ante preference for markets (a residue of the fact that economics developed alongside political individualism) and their concomitant belief that markets systematically punish "irrational" behavior plays a very important role in the Neoclassicals' analysis of foreign exchange rates.

In terms of specific modeling techniques, Neoclassical economists tend to rely heavily on deductivism (typically expressed mathematically) and equilibrium analysis. The former results from their implicit belief that less can be understood about economic activity from observing it than from the process of devising axiomatic first principles. In other words, while it may on some level be interesting to hear what managers claim to do in terms of pricing, there are reasons to suspect that their assertions are less than reliable and that we should instead suppose for them some simple and reasonable behavioral tendencies (e.g., short-term profit maximization). Our senses may deceive us (both as actors in the economy and as researchers), and we should thus depend instead on *reasoning* for inputs into our analyses. This process of developing first principles of economic behavior meshes well with the use of deductive logic in drawing conclusions from these behavioral and structural assumptions.[2]

Because mathematics is such a useful device in constructing and testing deductive arguments, it has become an important tool in the Neoclassical model. Every one of their major theories of international economics can be expressed mathematically; in fact, it is the preferred method. A series of relations or assumptions (derived, as suggested above, primarily from reasoning rather than observation) is quantified, and then conclusions are drawn by either solving for or manipulating variables in the system. It is probably safe to say that no new development would be taken seriously by the economic Neoclassical were it not expressed in this manner.

In addition, such deductive arguments are typically placed within an equilibrium framework. Economic phenomena are assumed to seek resting points from which they will not stray unless parameters within the model change or exogenous forces come to bear. The economy is thus characterized as timeless and static, with dynamics usually limited to simple comparisons of equilibrium positions.

Last, it is commonly assumed that there is a strong tendency toward continuous full employment.[3] The simplest version of this premise argues that demand can never fall short of total supply because the raison d'etre for supplying goods and services is to spend the income so earned. If that is so, then involuntary unemployment (beyond frictional and structural) falls to zero and the economy grows, without interruption, according to available resources and technology and past accumulation.[4] Though Neoclassical models allow for deviations from this ideal state, they are treated either as temporary (as in monetarism, where they represent short-run movements away from the natural rate) or due to "interference" with the natural tendencies of the economy (as in Neoclassical Keynesianism, where market rigidities like minimum wage laws and unions create downward wage rigidity). At the very least, they argue, full employment holds in the long run, a time horizon which in their view is determined by forces distinct from those relevant in the short run. Furthermore, according to Neoclassicism, it is to long-run analysis that we should look in informing policy.[5]

For exchange rate determination in such a world, it is fundamental that capital flows must play a passive role. In the long run, output and employment are wholly determined by technology, productivity, resources, and the stock of capital; there is, therefore, nothing left for the financial side of the economy to do but to adjust to the real sector (recall the simple Neoclassical macro model in Chapter One wherein the financial sector, via interest rates, acted to automatically reinvigorate spending). Financial capital flows in the Neoclassical model are an epiphenomenon. They arise and exist only because real economic activity took place. Money is neutral.

In summary, Neoclassical models, including those concerned with explaining exchange rate movements, are marked by a bias toward free-market solutions, a conspicuous lack of attention to historical and institutional detail, the assumption that economic forces tend toward equilibrium, axiomatic theorizing in a mathematical framework, and an almost complete lack of attention to the role of portfolio capital (due to the implicit acceptance of the long-run validity of the full employment assumption). Though I would argue that one can find elements of each of these in the theories reviewed below, it is the last that will be the most noticeable. Financial markets are either entirely ignored or of interest only because short-term "stickiness" or irrationality somewhere in the real economy is preventing rapid return to equilibrium. In the long run, they have no impact on the path that economic activity follows.

PURCHASING POWER PARITY[6]

The core Neoclassical exchange rate theory is purchasing power parity. It says in short that once exchange rates are taken into account the average price of goods and services world wide should be equal. That is:

$$\$/FX = P_\$/P_{FX} \qquad\qquad 2.1$$

where $\$/FX$ is the dollar price of foreign currency, $P_\$$ is the average price of goods and services in the United States, and P_{FX} is the average price of goods and services in the rest of the world. If this relationship does not hold, then (assuming no taxes, transportation, or transactions costs) it must be that merchandise is cheaper in one area than the other. This sets into motion arbitrage that will restore the equality (goods and services prices are bid up in the "cheap" nations and driven down in the "dear" nations, and the currencies of the "cheap" nations appreciate as agents buy those moneys to buy their products). In this way, it is implied that the trade balance drives the exchange rate and that there is a systemic tendency for balanced trade to emerge as the equilibrium (a recurring theme in Neoclassical models). Portfolio capital flows play no role in the theory of purchasing power parity.

Purchasing power parity is an extremely well-researched phenomenon. Econometric methods employed range from ordinary least squares to cointegration and data sets have included many countries around the world over long and varied time periods. Through all that, the best that economists can say is that there is *some* evidence that purchasing power parity *may* have validity for the major exchange rates over the long run (Sarno and Taylor 2002: 96). In the short run (where "short" implies three to five years), purchasing power parity is useless as a guide to currency price movements. Currency dealers go so far as to characterize the theory as "only academic jargon" (Cheung and Chinn 2000).

Why has such an intuitively appealing theory performed so poorly? Many suggestions have been made within the Neoclassical, ranging from measurement issues to nonlinearities. However, if financial flows are important, then the answer is quite simple (and overlooked): purchasing power parity assumes that trade flows dominate the foreign exchange market when in fact they do not; portfolio capital does. Take the data from Chapter One on currency markets, wherein the daily volume is sufficient to finance world trade over forty times.[7] Only if portfolio capital flows are white noise are they unimportant; otherwise, they clearly play a considerable role in driving currency prices. Purchasing power parity ignores them entirely, and one is not likely to successfully explain a phenomenon by focusing on a small, unrepresentative sample of its determinants.[8]

MONETARY MODEL

Though there is no single, universally accepted model of currency price determination among Neoclassical economists, the monetary model would probably at least claim the title of the most tested. It is, in essence, the monetarist approach to domestic macroeconomic modeling with purchasing power parity attached. In other words, the monetary model can be understood as equation 2.1 with a specific explanation of prices added.

Monetarism argues that prices are determined as follows:

$$P = MV/y \qquad\qquad 2.2$$

where P is the domestic price level, M is the supply of money, V is the velocity of money, and y is the level of real output. It is assumed that both V and y are constant (at least in the long run), V because they argue that it is a function of slow-to-change habits and institutions, y since the full employment assumption implies that it can only change either as supply shocks occur or due to the gradual growth of technology and population.[9] This leaves M as the sole long-run determinant of P.

Substituting 2.2 into 2.1:

$$\$/FX = (M_\$ V_\$/y_\$)/(M_{FX} V_{FX}/y_{FX}) \qquad\qquad 2.3$$

where all variables are as defined above and the subscripts indicate nationality (with FX used to represent the "foreign" country and $ the US or home country). Hence, the monetary approach argues that changes in the money supply lead to movements in the price level, which in turn causes exchange rate adjustments. Again, this is simply purchasing power parity with a specific explanation of prices tacked on.

Most versions of the monetary approach include interest rates as determinants of the exchange rate. One might be tempted to conclude that this means that capital flows are being taken into account. This is not the case, however, as rising domestic interest rates, for example, do not lead to what we observe in the real world: a domestic currency appreciation as international investors attempt to place more of the home country's bonds into their portfolio assets. Rather, their role is to affect the domestic demand for cash. What occurs when interest rates rise is a decline in the demand for cash (as agents move into bonds), leading to (assuming no change in the supply of money) an excess supply of cash and hence a rise in prices. Because this causes a deterioration in the trade balance, the home currency depreciates – precisely the opposite of what is observed in the real world. The developers of this model certainly did not have modern financial markets in mind when adding this feature.

The monetary model can be shown graphically as in Figure 2.1. On the left is the purchasing power parity (PPP) relationship. Measured on the vertical axis is the domestic (in this case, US) price level, and on the horizontal axis the price of foreign exchange in terms of dollars. As the slope of the PPP curve is the domestic price level divided by the exchange rate, if purchasing power parity holds it must be exactly equal to the foreign price level. If the foreign price level rises, the line is steeper, and vice versa. Note also that, first, an economy lying on the PPP curve must have balanced trade and, second, lying off the curve would set into motion the arbitrage discussed above (and hence move us back onto the curve). In particular, points to the right of PPP would imply a trade surplus for the domestic economy (leading to higher domestic prices and a domestic currency appreciation – both movements taking us back to PPP) and points to the left would imply a deficit (leading to falling domestic prices and a domestic currency depreciation; again movements returning the economy to PPP).

The graph on the right in Figure 2.1 is the domestic macroeconomy. The vertical axis remains the domestic price level, while the horizontal is real output or income.

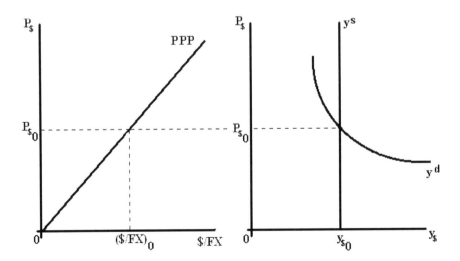

Figure 2.1 Monetary model setup.

In this simple version the aggregate supply curve is vertical at the full employment (or natural) level of real output. This can be termed the long-run supply curve and a more traditionally shaped positive short-run curve can be added as well (where the position of the latter is a function of workers' perceptions of the current price level). However, as this would only create further complication and not change the basic result of the model, the long-run, vertical-supply-curve version will be studied here.

Note that once the long-run supply curve is identified, the level of output is completely determined. Regardless of what else we show on either diagram in Figure 2.1, we know that $y = y_{\$0}$. No other outcome is possible and money and financial issues do not matter. The function y^s can shift, but this will tend to occur only over the long run as resources, technology, productivity, and the stock of capital change (for better or worse).

The demand curve (which exists in this model only to resolve the question of what the price level must be) is derived from equation 2.2 above:

$$P = MV/y \qquad\qquad 2.2$$

Given V as a constant and M as an exogenous variable under control of the central monetary authority, the demand curve is simply all the combinations of P and y (or in the case of Figure 2.1, $P_\$$ and $y_\$$) that solve equation 2.2. The demand curve asymptotically approaches either axis because neither P nor y can fall to zero and still satisfy an equation where V and M are non-zero. Changing either V or M will shift y^d (in particular, a rise in either necessitates a rightward shift).

Once we see where y^d intersects y^s, we know $P_\$$. Armed with $P_\$$ and assuming a particular price level in the foreign country (which defines the slope of PPP), the exchange rate is known. If shifts occur in PPP, y^d, or y^s, this will temporarily move us away from the PPP curve and lead to a trade deficit or surplus. The resulting arbitrage returns the system to equilibrium. For example, say the central monetary authority chooses to increase the money supply. This is illustrated in Figure 2.2, where the initial equilibria are at point $(P_{\$0}, (\$/FX)_0)$ on the PPP diagram and $(P_{\$0}, y_{\$0})$ on the domestic macroeconomy. If M then rises, all the combinations of P and y that solve equation 2.2 are at higher points, and therefore y^d shifts to the right. This raises $P_\$$ to $P_{\$1}$ (in terms of the behavior of the agents involved, they attempt to rid themselves of the excess money balances by spending but, because we are already at the full employment level and no more output can be forthcoming, this only bids prices higher).

Moving to the PPP diagram, the rise in the price level has placed the economy at point A, where the domestic economy (the US in this example) is experiencing a trade deficit. This means that domestic goods and services are not selling, while those of the trading partner are. Ceteris paribus, this will place downward pressure on the domestic price level, upward pressure on the foreign price level, and cause the domestic money to lose value. However, if we assume that neither national price level can change without a policy decision by their central bank (an assumption that can be relaxed if we allow for flows of money between the two nations – a

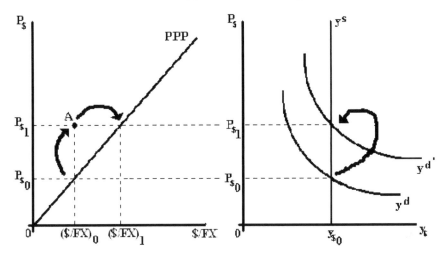

Figure 2.2 Monetary model, effects of an increase in the money supply.

necessity, incidentally, in the fixed exchange rate version of this model), then the only variable able to bear the burden of adjustment is the exchange rate. Hence, in Figure 2.2, the dollar will depreciate, falling from $(\$/FX)_0$ to $(\$/FX)_1$.[10]

As the graphical analysis drives home, the monetary approach is purchasing power parity (the graph on the left) with a few new features added (the graph on the right). As such, it suffers from all the former's weaknesses. In particular, it is based on the assumption that trade flows drive currency prices, and that trade flows are a function of price variables only. Though changes in income may have an impact in the short run (more sophisticated models use money illusion to allow agents to freely choose levels other than the full employment one until they realize that their choices were based on flawed perceptions), they do so only by changing the demand for cash and not because, as we so often observe in the real world, they raise import levels.

Not surprisingly, the empirical record of the monetary model is very similar to that of purchasing power parity. In general, it is possible to obtain some success for a few countries over the very long run (Rapach and Wohar 2002). But again, while it may be *suggestive* in terms of long-term movements, it is a poor guide to policy over the time horizons in which we live our lives.[11]

INTEREST RATE PARITY

Interest rate parity is associated with the work of Irving Fisher and the Fisher effect.[12] Most simply, it argues that the rate of return from holding interest-denominated assets must tend toward equality across countries. Interest rate parity comes in two forms: covered and uncovered. The latter appears below as equation 2.4:

$$(\$/FX)^e/(\$/FX) = (1+r_\$)/(1+r_{FX}) \qquad\qquad 2.4$$

where $(\$/FX)^e$ is the expected future spot exchange rate, $(\$/FX)$ is the current spot exchange rate, $r_\$$ is the rate of interest available on dollars, and r_{FX} is the rate of interest available on foreign currency.[13] If it is rearranged as shown in 2.4', its meaning becomes especially clear as it shows that the rate of return (plus principle) one could earn on an interest-bearing asset in the United States, $(1+r_\$)$, must be equal to the same amount translated into foreign currency (i.e., multiplied by $(FX/\$)$), earned (multiplied by $(1+r_{FX})$), and then repatriated (multiplied by $(\$/FX)^e$):

$$(1+r_\$) = (FX/\$)(1+r_{FX})(\$/FX)^e \qquad\qquad 2.4'$$

If for some reason the equality does not hold, then forces are set in motion which restore equilibrium. For example, were the left-hand side of 2.4' larger than the right, this would mean that agents expected the rate of return to be higher in the United States than elsewhere. This would attract capital into the US, driving $r_\$$ down, moving r_{FX} up, and causing a dollar appreciation (a rise in FX/$). This process continues until 2.4' (and by implication, 2.4) holds again.

Covered interest rate parity is superficially similar but has a very different meaning and consists entirely of observable variables. It is shown as equation 2.5:

$$(\$/FX)^f/(\$/FX) = (1+r_\$)/(1+r_{FX}) \qquad\qquad 2.5$$

where $(\$/FX)^f$ is the forward exchange rate (i.e., the price at which an agent, typically a bank, agrees in the present to deliver foreign currency at some date in the future), $(\$/FX)$ is the current spot exchange rate, $r_\$$ is the rate of interest available on dollars, and r_{FX} is the rate of interest available on foreign currency.[14] Not coincidentally, the equation bankers use to calculate the forward rate they will charge customers is simply 2.5 rearranged (Taylor 1987):

$$(\$/FX)^f = (\$/FX)((1+r_\$)/(1+r_{FX})) \qquad\qquad 2.5'$$

Essentially, their goal is to immediately cover any commitments created by a forward transaction by buying the necessary currency today. If the interest rate that the bank then earns in the foreign economy (while holding the currency until the delivery date) is lower than that at home, the bank makes up the loss by setting the forward rate at the premium indicated by 2.5'; if the foreign interest rate is higher, competitive pressures will force the bank to pass this excess on to the customer in the form of a discount, again determined by 2.5'. The bank earns its income either through transactions fees or the spread between the buy and sell rates.

Because, except for the substitution $(\$/FX)^f$ for $(\$/FX)^e$, this equation is identical to that for uncovered interest rate parity, some economists have argued that $(\$/FX)^f$ could serve as a proxy for $(\$/FX)^e$. It is especially tempting to believe this since the latter would be a very useful variable to obtain and yet is unobservable. And it is certainly true that if both covered and uncovered interest rate parity held then $(\$/FX)^f$ would be equal to $(\$/FX)^e$. Unfortunately, not only are $(\$/FX)^f$ and $(\$/FX)^e$ not created by similar processes, but while there is a great deal of evidence that covered interest rate parity holds, the record for uncovered is mixed at best (see Taylor 1987 for an example of the former and Wu 2007 for the latter). In fact, there are compelling reasons to believe that equation 2.4 does not represent an equilibrium relationship in the real world. The lengthy explanation of this contention is left for Chapter Five. Suffice it to say for now that agents' collective uncertainty regarding their forecasts opens the door to other factors determining the actual relationship between currency prices and interest rates. Covered interest rate parity holds because it is a definition rather than an equilibrium relationship; uncovered does not hold because it does not take into account the manner in which agents form expectations.

DORNBUSCH MODEL

In response to the obvious weaknesses of the monetary model, Rudiger Dornbusch proposed a new and innovative approach (Dornbusch 1976). The major differences were the rejection of the continuous maintenance of purchasing power parity and the explicit inclusion of uncovered interest rate parity as a determinant of currency prices.

The Dornbusch model makes a sharp distinction between short-run and long-run phenomena. Long-run outcomes are comparable to those found in the monetary model in that purchasing power parity holds and output returns to its natural level (or rate of growth, if the model is specified in logs). In fact, equations 2.2 and 2.3 above are included in the Dornbusch model, as are both of the graphs employed in Figures 2.1 and 2.2 (albeit with a few modifications). In the end, however, money and finance remain irrelevant.

In the short run, it is assumed that certain rigidities exist that prevent prices from fully responding to exogenous events. At the domestic level this means that the income variable is required to absorb the excess. Hence, the initial effect of a rise in the money supply, for example, would be a rise in *both* output and prices. This is modeled by allowing short-term fluctuations in y in equation 2.2, and by introducing an IS-LM apparatus into the system. The latter is necessary to link the change in y now permitted under the sticky price assumption to changes in the interest rate.[15] Once these are known, they can be plugged into the uncovered interest rate parity equation to determine the new exchange rate. The former is expressed as:

$$(\$/FX)^e/(\$/FX) = (1+r_s)/(1+r_{FX}) \qquad 2.4$$

where all variables are defined as above. According to the Dornbusch model, this must hold at all times.

The uncovered interest rate parity relationship can be shown graphically as in Figure 2.3. The exchange rate (domestic currency units per foreign currency unit) is shown on the horizontal axis and the interest rate in the home country is graphed on the vertical. Each UIRP function is drawn for a particular foreign interest rate (which can be recorded on the vertical) and expected exchange rate. Changing either will entail a shift (detailed below). It is easiest to begin with the point at which the domestic and foreign interest rates are the same. First, the UIRP shown is drawn assuming that agents expect the future spot rate to be equal to $(\$/FX)_0$ (hence the notation under the UIRP label). Second, recalling either equation 2.4 or 2.4', it is easily shown that if $r_s = r_{FX}$, then it must also be true that $(\$/FX)^e = (\$/FX)$. Hence, at the point where $r_s = r_{FX}$ on Figure 2.3, the prevailing exchange rate must also be the one that is expected by agents to prevail in the future: $(\$/FX)_0$. This must be the case since any excess expected return in either country would lead to compensating capital flows that eliminated the excess. If the rates

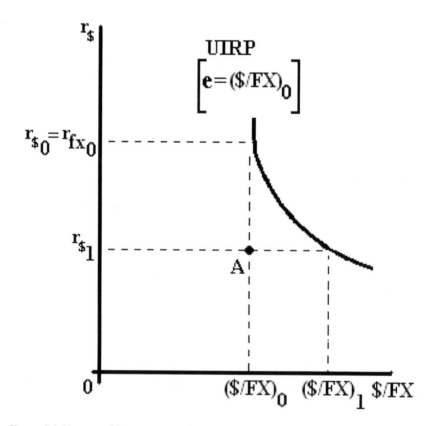

Figure 2.3 Uncovered interest rate parity.

of interest are identical, then agents cannot be expecting to earn extra return as a result of currency appreciation or depreciation.

Now assume a fall in the domestic rate of interest to r_{S1}. This leaves us at point A, where US assets are expected to earn a lower return than those in the rest of the world (this is easily seen by the fact that the exchange rate is already at the level the market expects to prevail in the future, but US interest rates are lower than Japanese). This leads to capital flows away from the US which will cause, ceteris paribus, a rise in r_S, a fall in r_{FX}, and a depreciation of the dollar (a rise in (\$/FX)). Making the interest rates exogenous and placing the entire burden of adjustment on the exchange rate yields the movement illustrated on Figure 2.3 to point (r_{S1}, (\$/FX)$_1$). This is an equilibrium position because even though US interest rates are lower than those in the rest of the world, agents expect the dollar to compensate by appreciating.

Were expectations to change then we would see a self-fulfilling prophecy in Figure 2.3. For example, if agents came to believe that the dollar would be cheaper in the future than they had earlier anticipated, UIRP would shift to the right. Having done so would leave the economy momentarily at a point to the left of the new UIRP, which is comparable to what occurred after the domestic interest rate movement in Figure 2.3. Just as there, the capital would flow out of the US and the dollar would depreciate as anticipated. Changing the foreign interest rate also requires a shift in UIRP, rightward for a rise and leftward for a fall. In any event, all points to the left of a particular UIRP imply a net capital outflow for the domestic country (leading to a domestic currency deprecation) and all points to the right of a particular UIRP imply a net capital inflow for the domestic country (leading to a domestic currency appreciation).

The IS-LM portion of the construct can be expressed as in equations 2.6 through 2.10:

$$S = (r, y) \tag{2.6}$$
$$+ +$$

$$I = (r) \tag{2.7}$$
$$-$$

$$S = I \tag{2.8}$$

$$M^d/P = (r, y) \tag{2.9}$$
$$- +$$

$$M^d/P = M^s/P \tag{2.10}$$

where S is savings, r is the interest rate, y is real output, I is investment, M^d/P is (real) money demand, and M^s/P is (real) money supply. Equations 2.6 through 2.8 specify IS (the first two giving behavioral relationships and the last showing the equilibrium condition) and equations 2.9 and 2.10 specify LM (with 2.9 showing the money demand equation and 2.10 the equilibrium condition; nominal money supply is assumed exogenous). To this simple version, a government and trade sector are added so that 2.8 becomes:

$$S = I + (G - T) + B \qquad\qquad 2.8'$$

where G is government spending, T is taxes, and B is the current account balance. The last is assumed to be a positive function of the real exchange rate, Q:

$$Q = (\$/FX)(P_{FX}/P_\$) \qquad\qquad 2.11$$

where all variables are defined as above. Note that when purchasing power parity holds, it must be true that $\$/FX = P_\$/P_{FX}$ and, therefore, $Q = 1$.

The IS-LM apparatus is represented graphically in Figure 2.4. Real output or income is measured along the horizontal axis and the interest rate along the vertical. The IS curve is the locus of points that shows the combinations of interest and output that set injections into the income stream equal to leakages. At the most

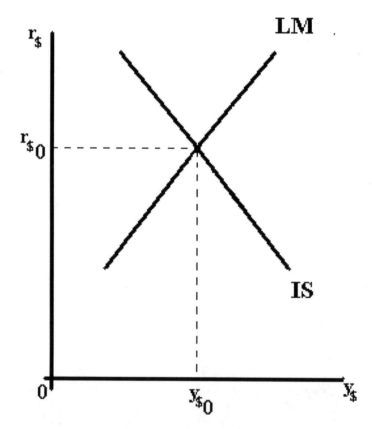

Figure 2.4 IS-LM curves.

basic level that means I = S. Equation 2.8', however, captures better what will need to be modeled here:

$$S = I + (G - T) + B \hspace{8cm} 2.8'$$

Of these variables, G and T are exogenous and B will be a function of the real exchange rate, Q. Only S and I are driven by determinants measured on the axes. Taking any particular point in the space as satisfying equation 2.8, assume a rise in interest rates. Will this necessitate a rise or fall in real output and income? Rising interest rates have no effect on G, T, or B, but cause S to increase and I to fall (see equations 2.6 and 2.7). This would lead to leakages exceeding injections, causing a recession. Consequently, y will fall and, along with it, S (see equation 2.6). This fall will continue until S declines sufficiently to re-establish the equality of leakages and injections. The lesson here is that rising interest rates require a fall in y, so IS is negatively sloped. Changes in G, T, and B will cause a shift, with rising G and B moving the function to the right and rising T to the left.

The LM curve is the locus of points that shows the combinations of interest and output that set the real supply of money equal to the real demand for money. Again, take any random point as satisfying equation 2.10. Now arbitrarily raise real output to see what impact this will have on the money market. According to equation 2.9, the demand for money will rise. However, with no change in the supply, this means there is a shortage. Bankers will response by raising interest rates in an effort to both attract more deposits and ration the funds that are available. In the money market, each time y rises, so must r. The LM curve therefore has positive slope.

To show how the equation-based model works, assume a rise in the money supply (both nominal and real). In the long run, the only result will be as has been shown in the monetary model: a rise in the domestic price level and a depreciation of the home currency (with trade remaining balanced). In the interim, however, a number of events occur. To begin, when M rises in equation 2.2, both P and y rise (recall that V is constant). The rise in y is reflected in the IS-LM system. In that instance it occurs not because the excess supply of money is spent, driving prices higher and temporarily raising output over its natural level or rate (the explanation consistent with equation 2.2), but due to the fact that the monetary policy stimulus lowers interest rates and thereby raises investment and consumption. This occurs via equations 2.9, 2.7, and 2.6. Note that the rise in investment and consumption does not create an additional rise in y, but is simply the IS-LM equivalent of that which takes place in equation 2.2.

The fall in the domestic interest rate now impacts on the price of foreign currency. Though it is clear from equation 2.4 that the fall in the US interest rate will lead to a depreciation of the spot dollar, there is a complicating factor (which is the key to the novelty of this approach). The increase in the money supply will have signaled to investors, equipped with rational expectations, a long-run change in the exchange rate. Furthermore, they will assume that change is equivalent to the one the monetary model would predict.[16] Hence, the estimates embodied in

($/FX)^e will have been revised upward by *exactly* the amount implied by equation 2.2 (given a constant V and y); and because of the relationship specified in equation 2.4, ($/FX) will have to rise by the same amount as ($/FX)^e (at this stage it is assumed that neither r has reacted). *This adjustment in expectations and the spot price of currency occurs immediately after the increase in the money supply.* It is the very first thing that happens and, in the end, this movement will represent the only permanent change in the exchange rate. But in the meantime there will be an additional decline in the dollar caused by the interest rate fall. It represents *overshooting* and will correct once the economy returns to long-run equilibrium (and r falls back to its original level). It occurs precisely because of the price rigidity that led to the increase in y reflected in IS-LM. Had the price rise been proportional to the money supply increase, LM would not have shifted (since the real money supply would not have changed) and the interest rate would not have moved. There would have been no overshooting.

But the US interest rate does fall so that the value of the dollar has moved below its long-run equilibrium – an equilibrium that is still, as in the monetary model, equivalent to the purchasing power parity value of the dollar – meaning that the US will run a trade surplus (this also causes a rightward shift in IS, further raising y; the consequent rise in r is assumed to be smaller than the initial fall). All the while, prices are continuously, if slowly, moving to their long-run equilibrium levels.[17] As this process plays itself out, the real money supply declines (shifting LM to the left) and the real exchange rate falls (shifting IS to the left). This combination lowers y and (by assumption, since it could move in either direction) raises r. Given that uncovered interest rate parity holds constantly, the rise in r must lead to a dollar appreciation.[18] This continues, with y falling, r rising, and ($/FX) falling, until purchasing power parity is again satisfied and excess demand in the domestic economy is relieved. Long-run equilibrium is achieved and only P and ($/FX) have moved.

The graphic version of this sequence of events is illustrated in Figure 2.5. Note first the addition of several notations on the graphs and a short-run aggregate supply curve on the monetary model's macro diagram in the bottom right quadrant. Beginning with the latter, the vertical aggregate supply curve from Figure 2.2 is now the long-run supply curve y^s (l.r.). Real output will eventually return to y_{s0}, but it may deviate in the short run. This is shown by the horizontal y^s (s.r.), or short-run aggregate supply curve. Such a curve exists, it is assumed, because prices are sticky in the short run which temporarily forces the entire burden of adjustment onto y. With respect to notation, the y^s-y^d diagram and IS-LM have parenthetical references to the variables that will shift those functions in this example (others may be added, as implied by the mathematical functions used to derive them). LM, for example, shows M/P$_\$$, or the real money supply. As it rises, this will shift LM to the right and hence drive interest rates down. IS shows Q which is defined above as the real exchange rate.[19] It is the true cost of foreign goods and services (with both the nominal exchange rate and relative price levels taken into account). As Q rises, so foreign goods and services become more expensive and a trade surplus is experienced by the domestic economy. This causes injections to exceed

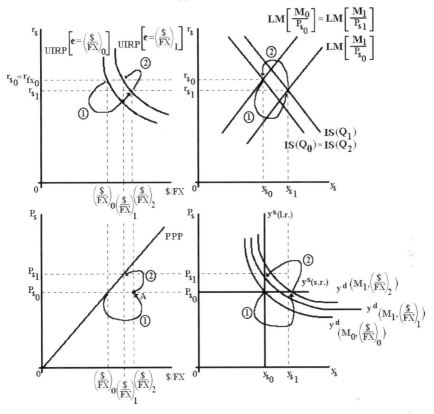

Figure 2.5 Dornbusch model, effects of an increase in the money supply.

leakages at any of the combinations of r and y available on the current IS, so IS must shift to the right. This leaves all the injections unaffected, but the rise in y causes a leakage (S) to increase. Equilibrium is restored. Finally, y^d is shifted by two variables: the money supply (as was already true in the monetary model) and the nominal exchange rate. As explained earlier, a rise in the money supply shifts y^d to the right, and in the Dornbusch model it will be assumed that a rise in $/FX (a domestic currency depreciation) also leads to a rightward shift.[20]

Showing the effect of a rise in the money supply (as was traced mathematically above) proceeds as follows. The initial equilibrium is given by all the variables subscripted with a zero. Now suppose the central monetary authority raises the money supply (and that they make no secret of this fact). Agents become aware of the policy move and the very first impact is on their expectations. As stated above, they have rational expectations and believe that the monetary model will prevail over the long run. Hence, they immediately decide that the future spot rate will come to rest at $(\$/FX)_1$ (they know that this is the right level because when purchasing power parity holds it is the equilibrium exchange rate for the final rise in the price level to $P_{\$1}$).

The change in agents' expectations requires a shift in UIRP to the curve where $e = (\$/FX)_1$. Given the fact that neither interest rate has changed (and nor may they without shifts in their corresponding IS-LM diagrams – the entire burden of adjustment in the UIRP market is on the spot exchange rate), the spot rate must immediately move to the level agents expect: $(\$/FX)_1$. All this has occurred in the rapidly adjusting financial market. Nothing so far has had time to happen anywhere else in the model.[21]

Now imagine the impact of the domestic currency depreciation and the rise in the money supply on the IS-LM diagram. Given that neither domestic nor foreign prices have moved, there is a rightward shift in both functions. While this will clearly lead to a rise in y, the effect on r is ambiguous; it is assumed to fall, however. Following the arrow labeled "1" on the IS-LM apparatus leads us to point $(r_{\$1}, y_{\$1})$ (actually, just short of that, since there is about to be an additional currency price depreciation that will move IS a little further to the right). Now move to the UIRP diagram, where there has been both a shift and a movement down the horizontal axis. This leaves the new exchange rate as $(\$/FX)_2$. Dropping down to PPP – which need not hold in the short run – the combination of $(\$/FX)_2$ and $P_{\$0}$ (which has yet to adjust) puts us off PPP to the right at point A. The US is experiencing a trade surplus because the dollar depreciation overshot its long-run equilibrium. Finally, the current situation on the y^d-y^s diagram is shown by the intersection between the short-run y^s and the y^d labeled with M_1 and $(\$/FX)_2$ (note that it is shifted higher than the long-run equilibrium y^d because of the overshooting exchange rate). The short-run movements end here, at $r_{\$1}$, $y_{\$1}$, $P_{\$0}$, and $(\$/FX)_2$.

The next stage of the process (all the arrows labeled with a "2") begins as price finally adjusts. To see the impact of this movement begin again on IS-LM. First, it is clear that both IS and LM will shift left, the former because Q is falling and the latter because M/P is doing the same. How far will IS and LM move? Back to their original levels. This must be true because PPP holds in the long run (putting Q back to 1) and, with y back to the natural rate as defined by the long run supply curve, equation 2.2 shows that M and P must have changed proportionally (so that their ratio is unchanged). We return on IS-LM to $r_{\$0}$, $y_{\$0}$. With $r_\$$ back to $r_{\$0}$ on UIRP, the exchange rate must have moved to $(\$/FX)_1$ (just as agents predicted it would – note that this appreciation also helps to push IS back to its original position). The change in $/FX shifts y^d down slightly, and the price level associated with the new demand curve (as it intersects with long run supply) will combine with $(\$/FX)_1$ in a manner that restores purchasing power parity. In the end, only three variables have changed in the model: the exchange rate, the expected exchange rate, and the price level.

On the surface of it, the Dornbusch model is a significant improvement over the monetary approach, especially in that it seems to offer a more dynamic view with an active portfolio capital market and the possibility of fluctuations in output above and below the natural rate.[22] But while the Dornbusch model does represent a step forward, some of this progress is more apparent than real. For example, capital flows occur only as a result of government policy or a supply shock. They react, but they do not cause; nor is their impact lasting or able to truly affect the economy. This is directly attributable to the full employment (or natural rate) assumption – output always returns to the same level or rate of growth, so there is no opening for finance to affect real variables.

Second, while certainly superior to the monetarist portrayal, the dynamism is somewhat contrived. Rather than a wholesale shift to modeling in historical time, where the past has a qualitative effect on the future, it is still mechanical. We know as soon as the increase in the money supply takes place where we will end up – it's only a matter of how long it will take. In other words, the future is not path dependent, it is pre-determined.

Last, the fluctuations above and below the natural rate in no way represent a break from the full employment assumption. Rigidities exist that prevent it from working properly, but it is still there. And eventually, it wins out. Regardless of the size of any change in the money supply, sooner or later the economy will return to the long-run natural rate of growth.

Still, there is an explicit provision made for the role of expectations in the determination of currency prices, which was certainly a step in the right direction. In fact, once the change is made in money supply, the first movement of the exchange rate is due solely to a change in agents' forecasts. Unfortunately, the assumption of rational expectations completely eliminates the chance of $(\$/FX)^e$ playing any role other than to passively accommodate the economy's movement toward long-run equilibrium.[23] To better understand its place in the model, consider what would happen if expectations did not adjust after a money supply change.

There is no rightward shift in UIRP but, as before, when M rises in equation 2.2, both P and y rise. A matching increase in y occurs in the IS-LM system as interest rates fall and investment and consumption are encouraged. According to equation 2.4, the fall in $r_\$$ means there must be a depreciation of the dollar. Given that there has been no change in either national price level, this means that purchasing power parity no longer holds and the US is running a trade surplus. This causes a rightward shift of IS (due to the rise in Q), but not so large that there is not still a net decline in US interest rates. This completes the short-term movements.

In the long run, prices will begin to adjust. As this occurs, LM will move back to its original position. Since y must also return to its starting point, then IS must too. And if both IS and LM have returned, then $r_\$$ cannot have changed.

But the fact that $(\$/FX)^e$ has not changed due to a shift in UIRP (as before) creates an irreconcilable problem in the model. Recall equation 2.4:

$$(\$/FX)^e/(\$/FX) = (1+r_\$)/(1+r_{FX}) \qquad\qquad 2.4$$

Expectations have not changed, $r_\$$ has returned to its original level, and r_{FX} is exogenous and unchanged. Therefore, if uncovered interest rate parity must hold at all times, as required by the Dornbusch model, then $(\$/FX)$ must also be at its original level. But that means that since $P_\$$ rose but neither $\$/FX$ nor P_{FX} have changed, purchasing power parity does not hold even in the long run (and the US has a trade deficit). The model breaks down. Without making the powerful assumption that agents believe the Monetary model drives long run exchange rates (and that they have rational expectations), UIRP and PPP cannot both hold in the long run. Also, despite the fact that the model no longer operates as intended, agents' expectations were correct! They did not expect the exchange rate to move and, assuming UIRP holds continuously and given that r_s returns to its original level, that is precisely what happened. Interestingly, the latter would hold true regardless of the expectational assumptions made. This is so because, first, given an increase in the money supply, IS and LM must always return to their original positions in the Dornbusch model. The real money supply will be unchanged in the long run, and the fact that y can change only temporarily means that IS must move back. Hence, r_s cannot move. As r_{FX} is fixed and $(\$/FX)^e$ is exogenous, this means that $(\$/FX)$ always moves to match the expectations of economic agents. Only if the latter happen to coincide with the level that would yield purchasing power parity will trade return to balance. That is precisely the purpose of the Dornbusch model's assumptions regarding $(\$/FX)^e$. That is a shame, as the model would be considerably more interesting and relevant if expectations were allowed a free role rather than being tied to proving the monetary model's case.[24] The Post Keynesian model developed in Chapter Five will not share this weakness.

THE MEESE AND ROGOFF CRITIQUE AND SURVEY STUDIES

Though none of the above models tested terribly well, there was faith in the underlying truth of the relationships as modeled, at least over the long run. However, a truly remarkable paper was published in 1983 that broke (at least on the surface) with this thinking. Richard Meese and Kenneth Rogoff, young staffers at the International Monetary Fund, were charged with determining which of the extant exchange rate models generated the best forecast (Rogoff 2001). To their surprise, nothing could outperform a model based on the simple premise that today's spot price is a predictor of tomorrow's spot price (a random walk).[25] The initial response to their controversial results was decidedly negative. Robert Clower, the editor of the *American Economic Review*, for example, "sent our manuscript back in return mail with a scathing letter saying that the results are obviously garbage and if we wish to remain in the economics profession, we had better develop a more positive attitude" (Rogoff 2001: 4). Still, eventually they *were* published and the implications of the study could not be ignored (see Meese and Rogoff 1983).

Whether Meese and Rogoff's results were a function of the fact that the large-scale models were simply wrong or because they had (in the Neoclassical view) unfairly tested the short-term forecasting abilities of what were essentially long-term processes, they encouraged a shift in the focus of empirical studies. Economists began testing currency market characteristics rather than complete models of foreign exchange rate determination. In particular, the assumptions of rationality and efficiency were questioned. This new research program was not solely a function of the Meese/Rogoff results. The early 1980's were also witness to a dramatic rise in the availability of surveys of exchange market participants' forecasts of future spot rates.[26] Hence, it was possible to undertake hitherto impossible studies. Still, given the suspicion with which Neoclassicals view survey data, Meese and Rogoff (1983) was probably necessary if not sufficient; this ushered in a decade of tests involving exchange market expectations.

Most popular were tests for rationality and efficiency. These are rather straightforward as an economist need only be armed with spot currency data and a set of currency forecasts. For example, the following could be used to test for rational expectations:

$$(\$/FX)_{t+k} = \alpha + \delta E_t(\$/FX)_{t+k} + e_{t+k} \qquad\qquad 2.12$$

where $(\$/FX)_{t+k}$ is the spot price of foreign currency (in dollars) in period t+k, $E_t(\$/FX)_{t+k}$ is the forecast in period t of the spot rate for period t+k, and e_{t+k} is a random error term. The forecast is unbiased (i.e., rational) if $\alpha = 0$ and $\delta = 1$.

One can extend this test of market participants' expectation-formation process by taking e_{t+k} from equation 2.12 and placing it into the following:

$$e_{t+k} = \beta + \lambda I_t + u_{t+k} \qquad\qquad 2.13$$

where I_t is information available in time t (researchers commonly use lagged values of e_{t+k} or the change in the exchange rate from t-1 to t as a proxy) and u_{t+k} is a random error term.[27] If the market is efficient there should be no relationship between the forecast error term e_{t+k} and the information that had been available at time period t. Hence, it is expected that $\beta = \lambda = 0$.

Many such tests have been conducted and there now exists widespread evidence that short-term forecasts are biased and markets are inefficient (Harvey 1998–9).[28] In other words, it appears that agents' predictions contain persistent errors that could have been corrected using existing information. The rising popularity of technical analysis had already put market efficiency under fire and this now added fuel to the fire.

BACK TO FUNDAMENTALS

Around the same time as the rise in popularity of survey-based studies, there was a conspicuous increase in the frequency with which currency price determinants were referenced as the "fundamentals" (see Harvey 2001 for an extensive discussion of this issue). This was a direct consequence of the troubles experienced in constructing empirical explanations of exchange rate movements (both large-scale models and tests of market efficiency and rational expectations). Identifying the determinants of currency prices in this general (and often quite vague) manner was a convenient mechanism for discussing the broader issues involved without getting bogged down in details.[29]

On the one hand, this is an intelligent strategy. Given the state of empirical exchange rate research, referencing the determinants in a more general manner makes sense. Why call them "money supply, output, and prices" or "the monetary model," for example, when there is little evidence that any specific list or model is the correct one? Strangely enough, however, that is, precisely what Neoclassical economists do when they offer a definition of the fundamentals. It is, in fact, common practice to explain the fundamentals by associating them with a list of specific variables or a particular currency price model. The advantage of the generalized approach is thus completely lost. To make matters worse, that is generally the extent of any attempt to define the fundamentals. There does not exist a single, coherent explanation of the concept; instead, readers are offered indirect references or definitions by example. This passage from Keith Pilbeam is typical: "economic fundamentals (are) derived from modern exchange rate models" (parenthetical reference added; Pilbeam 1994: 66). Were there a single, accepted approach to foreign exchange rate determination then this would be a clear statement. Of course, it would then also be unnecessary to call these determinants the fundamentals! Definitions by example, such as the one below by Mark Taylor, are similarly impractical, but common:

> The aim of this paper is to assess the importance of macroeconomic fundamentals – such as money supply, output, interest rates, and so on – for exchange rate movements and in particular for the modelling of exchange rate movements.
>
> (Taylor 1995b: 1)

Such an approach, lacking as it does a means for the reader to determine *why* Mark Taylor considers money supply, output, and interest rates as fundamentals, is of very limited usefulness.[30] A third approach, the least specific of all, is to say that the fundamentals are those variables "predicted by economic theory" as opposed to any specific model (MacDonald and Taylor 1992: 25).

What is it that Neoclassical economists mean by the fundamentals? As there is no apparent disagreement among them regarding their various definitions, one must assume that they perceive commonalities. Indeed, a careful reading of the literature reveals that what is generally meant by the fundamentals is "that set of variables guaranteeing the efficient operation of the foreign currency market" (Harvey 2001: 4). In other words, Neoclassical economists are assuming that whatever the fundamentals are specifically, in general they are the determinants that would (if they prevailed) generate efficient or optimal outcomes in the currency market. The fundamentals thus appear to become the foreign exchange equivalent of perfect competition – a market ideal rather than a description.

Again, this starts off sounding like a good idea. It is not unreasonable for economists to describe an ideal state in the market and then use that description as a template for devising policy prescriptions. However, they take the gigantic leap of *assuming* that the fundamentals serve not only as a theoretical ideal, but a representation of the real world as well. A priori, there is no justification for such a position. Furthermore, why should we, as social scientists, expect the phenomena we study to automatically generate best, or even second best, outcomes (something that seems to afflict economists much more so than our colleagues in the other social sciences)? The particular manner in which the world really works is largely independent of our wishes.[31]

Today, exchange rate theory is marked by a return to the models being studied 30 years ago. The difference is that there is not now any expectation that these have relevance in the short run. Since the latter is thought to be characterized by irrationalities and inefficiencies, some Neoclassical economists have decided that "economics" is simply not equipped to explain it. Hence, rather than seeking new tools, the discipline has redefined the subject of its analysis. Keynes' criticism of long-run analysis seems to be as relevant as ever.

FUNDAMENTALISTS VS. CHARTISTS AND MICROSTRUCTURE

It would be unfair to say that all Neoclassical economists have completely abandoned the short run or any attempt to develop new tools. Some work has been interesting. For example, Jeffrey Frankel and Kenneth Froot (1986) have suggested an approach which assumes three agents:

1   chartists: those forecasting currency prices by relying solely on autoregressive technical trading rules;
2   fundamentalists: those forecasting currency prices using exchange rate models (they suggest the Dornbusch) "that would be exactly correct if there were no chartists in the world" (Frankel and Froot 1986: 24); and,
3   portfolio managers: those who buy and sell foreign assets based on the expectations of the above two sets of agents.

The key to the model is the fact that portfolio managers weight the sets of forecasts based on whose has been the most accurate over the recent past. Frankel and Froot also allow for the possibility that chartists and fundamentalists are really the same people, shifting their primary focus under varying sets of circumstances (something that would fit well with the survey findings of Mark Taylor and Helen Allen (1992)). We witness the largest movements away from fundamental equilibrium, they argue, when there has been a regime change and portfolio managers are slow to learn the new model.

This is a superior approach to that taken in the full-scale models reviewed above. It takes into account the important role of charting and technical analysis and it does not assume that all agents' forecasts are characterized by rational expectations. Market participants must learn how the world works, a problematic undertaking given that the world evolves. Still, in the end it does not represent a clear break with the Dornbusch, monetary, and portfolio balance models. Consider this question: if portfolio managers set the foreign exchange rate via their buying and selling of currency, why do they bother changing their forecasts? Will they not always, in aggregate, be correct? Not in Frankel and Froot's model, because the process that determines exchange rates is assumed to be the following:

$$s_t = c\Delta s^m_{t+1} + z_t \qquad\qquad\qquad 2.14$$

where s_t is the spot exchange rate (logged), Δs^m_{t+1} is the rate of depreciation expected by portfolio managers, and z_t "represents other contemporaneous determinants" (Frankel and Froot 1986: 29). The variable z_t is shorthand for the fundamentals, which is represented by one of the traditional exchange rate models (or a derivative thereof). Hence, in the end it is still the fundamentals that drive currency prices. Indeed, the particular specification upon which Frankel and Froot depend in their 1986 paper is one wherein the fundamentals are proxied by the current account. Hence, though it is by far one of the most interesting Neoclassical approaches, it is still not a clean break with the premise that the financial side of the economy has no real impact. It is purchasing power parity in disguise.

Another innovative approach within the Neoclassical is typified by the work of Mark D. Flood (1994). Flood builds a simulation model of the foreign exchange market with the goal of "examining the market structure: the absolute and relative proportions of market-makers, brokers, and customers constituting the market" (Flood 1994: 132). He makes no assumption whatsoever regarding the relative importance of trade and capital flows, preferring instead to treat exogenous inputs as simply "news." Flood then specifies the structure of the market and the reaction functions of each agent. It is a very unique approach.

What his model suggests is that the unwanted inventories created by certain currency market events are not quickly or easily resolved. Rather, they are passed from agent to agent, creating further disruption and leading to market inefficiencies. Flood concludes that a means of centralizing price information would help resolve these problems.

ORDER FLOW

Last to be mentioned here is order flow. The basic idea is that asset prices react to buying pressure, or "the net of buyer-initiated and seller-initiated orders" (Evans and Lyons 2002: 171). This seems like a reasonable statement and, in fact, a rather elementary one. In the paper cited above, the exchange rate is modeled as a function of both the buying pressure variable (taken from Reuters data on Deutsche Mark/dollar and yen/dollar for four months of 1996) and the interest-rate differential. In short, this combination is shown to have an explanatory power far superior to that of other mainstream models.

But what does that ad hoc empirical approach really tell us? It shows that interest rates are important, which is entirely consistent with the Post Keynesian view that capital flows are key. The order flow variable itself, however, simply states that when more people want to buy than sell, price rises. The begging question, of course, is why that occurred. One attempt to answer this comes from Gradojevic and Neeley (2008), who examine the US-Canadian dollar market and test economic announcements as an explanation for variations in order flow. They are able to claim some significant successes.

This new approach breaks strongly with the Neoclassical bias toward real, fundamental variables as the driving force behind currency movements and it will be very interesting to see how the order-flow literature affects mainstream exchange rate research. Likely as not, it will be relegated to the remote fringes of mainstream economics, the short run. In the meantime, nothing in the buying-pressure argument is at odds with Post Keynesian economics.

CONCLUSIONS

To say that nothing has been learned from the above would be false. Those cited above are leading scholars in our discipline and their work has certainly pushed back the frontiers of our knowledge. Still, it does not matter how clever you are if one of your major premises is false. Their implicit acceptance of continuous full employment and consequent relegation of the financial sector to irrelevance dooms their investigations. Unless capital flows are white noise, their approach is, at best, misleading.

One of the strange features of the Neoclassical literature is that on occasion someone will raise the possibility that their basic premise with respect to the centrality of trade flows in driving exchange rates is wrong. See, for example, Ronald MacDonald:

> ... it is our contention that for a sample period such as the current float, net capital flows will not go to zero and, therefore, they should be explicitly recognized in modeling the measure of the long-run exchange rate currently adopted in the literature.
>
> (MacDonald 1995: 482)

No one has pursued these leads. It appears that if an answer is to be found, it is not going to arise from the Neoclassical approach.

3 Psychology and decision-making in the foreign exchange market[1]

Here begins the process of building the Post Keynesian alternative, something that will continue through Chapter Five. By then, a formal model will have been developed whose features include equilibrium trade imbalances, less-than-full employment, endogenous money, exchange rates marked by volatility and bandwagon effects, and an explanation of market participants' forecasts wherein expectations are guided by a mental model that is shaped by social forces. The goal of this chapter is to examine the institutional structure of global currency markets and the social and psychological factors affecting market participants' forecasting and decision making. Among the phenomena explained will be volatility, bandwagon effects, and forecast-construction bias. Reference will be made to Institutionalism, Keynes' *General Theory*, and the psychological research of Kahneman and Tversky.[2]

THE INSTITUTION OF FOREIGN CURRENCY TRADING

The first step in understanding the currency markets must be a review of their organization. Agents participating in the market for foreign exchange enter at one of three levels: wholesale (or market making), retail, or commercial. These are illustrated in Figure 3.1. Those acting in the top box are willing to make two-way offers on a continuous basis, such that they stand ready to buy *and* sell the currencies in which they offer wholesaling services. Agents operating at the wholesale or retail level may contact a wholesaler and request prices for a currency. Both a buy and sell rate will be quoted by the wholesaler before the caller reveals their intention. The caller then decides whether or not they will carry out their transaction at the price offered. The goal of the wholesaler is to "generate revenues from the *spread* between the offer and the bid" (Shoup 1998: 105), or the difference between the buy and sell prices. Because spreads at this level will be very small, wholesaling depends on generating volume to create income. Banks and other large financial institutions capable of maintaining well-staffed and equipped currency trading rooms with the liquidity necessary to maintain large inventories are typically the only ones willing to offer this service.

Retailing involves making one-way offers. Within the context of a particular transaction, those so acting are willing only to buy *or* sell a particular money. They

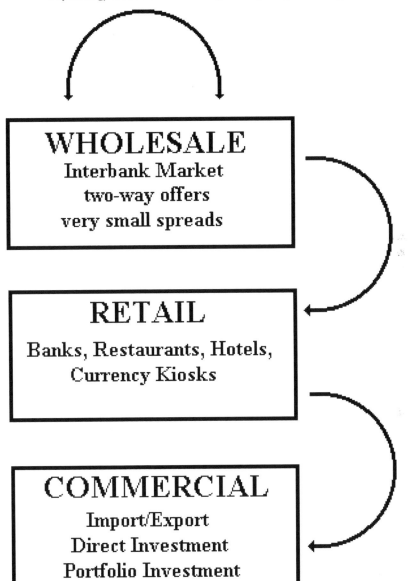

Figure 3.1 Foreign currency market structure.

purchase their funds from an agent who is wholesaling (who will, as indicated on Figure 3.1, offer two-way prices to the retailer) and then generate their income by selling at a mark-up to their customers (as indicated by the link between Retail and Commercial in Figure 3.1). Branch banks, restaurants, and hotels commonly undertake retailing.[3.4]

Those acting commercially are importers, direct investors, and portfolio investors.[5] Importers buy (or contract to buy) foreign currency because they wish to purchase foreign goods or services.[6] Direct investment is long-term capital investment abroad, such as the establishment of a multinational subsidiary or the purchase of a significant interest in some foreign firm. Portfolio-capital investors purchase the currencies necessary for the acquisition of the international financial assets (including deposits of the money itself and any associated interest income) they want to add to their portfolios. It is assumed that such purchases involve no long-term commitment on the part of the buyer and have as their goal short-run capital gain.

A single agent could undertake activities at all three levels (wholesale, retail, and commercial) at various times or in various markets or currencies. A financial institution could, for instance, operate in the wholesale market at one moment, supply funds to customers at the retail level in another, and engage in portfolio investment activities as a commercial actor in yet another. Playing multiple roles has the potential to afford such agents a competitive advantage since they can internalize some of the costs. That large institutions might be best placed to do this means that there is a potential for concentration in the market for foreign currency. Indeed, the 2002 Bank for International Settlements report on foreign exchange activity has reported trends consistent with this possibility:

> The consolidation trend in the banking industry that started in the mid-1990s appears to have continued between 1998 and 2001 … In the United States, 75% of forex market transactions were conducted by only 13 banks in 2001 compared to 20 banks in 1998 and about 20 banks in 1995. In the United Kingdom, 17 banks captured 75% of the market in 2001 compared to 24 banks in 1998 and about 20 banks in 1995.
>
> (BIS 2002: 9)

There is evidence that market participants sense this well, as shown in Cheung and Chinn (2000). Their survey of currency dealers indicates that for the big four currency rates, 17 percent thought that there were dominant players in the dollar-Deutsche Mark market, 22 percent in the dollar-yen, 50 percent on the dollar-sterling, and over 58 percent in the dollar-Swiss franc. The reasons survey respondents supposed that such agents could dominate were related primarily to sheer size.

CURRENCY MARKET PARTICIPANTS' ROLES

Prices in the foreign exchange market are negotiated among market participants on a continuous basis. As few rigidities or externalities exist, the question of what determines the exchange rate becomes what determines the relative demands for currencies? To answer this requires a closer look at wholesaling, retailing, and commercial demands.

The effect of retailing is relatively minor. Retailers merely intermediate between commercial actors and wholesalers, charging a mark up in the process. This means that retailing has no independent impact on the currency market. They act in response to their customers' demand and earn income from the mark-up they charge.

The act of wholesaling is more complicated. Because they earn their income on the narrow spread between bid and ask prices, they must quote prices that they *anticipate* will generate an equal volume of business on both sides of the market. If they are incorrect, then their inventories of currencies accumulate in a way that creates for them a vested interest in future exchange rate movements. For example, if a currency-trading desk set a price that attracted more sell orders for the yen than buy orders, it would accumulate large inventories of that currency. In that case, they would rather not witness a yen depreciation! Wholesalers by definition want to earn risk-free profits by "jobbing." It is not their goal to engage in currency speculation and thus quoting a price that will leave working inventories unaffected is a central goal.

Doing so is not simple. As the currency desk receives orders over the course of the day, the wholesaler must decide whether the timing of the orders is coincident or the result of unexpected trends (Suvanto 1993: 1–22). If it is the former and, in fact, the price the wholesaler is quoting will (by the close of business) leave her with a closed position (i.e., without unintended inventory accumulation), then the fact that the morning happened to be witness to an excess of orders for the euro, for example, should not lead her to change her bid or offer. But, if it is determined that the unexpected demand for the euro is a function of an actual shift in market sentiment then the price at which the euro is sold must be increased if desired inventories are to be maintained. Thus, it is incumbent upon wholesalers to make careful forecasts of customer demands (something that is not necessary in the more passive act of retailing). That greater sophistication is required to wholesale is the reason that large banks and investment firms are usually the only agents in a position to do so (they will also almost certainly be among those firms with oligopoly power referenced above).[7] Despite this greater complication, however, wholesaling has roughly the same impact on prices as retailing even if more steps may be involved. They are only acting in response to changes that have taken place (or that they anticipate) at the commercial level. It is, therefore, from the latter that the ultimate demand for currency arises, and thus where exchange rates are determined.[8]

As suggested above, there are three basic sets of commercial demands for foreign currency: those arising from imports, from the demand for direct foreign investment abroad, and from the demand for portfolio investment abroad. A rise in any one of those will increase the demand for and (ceteris paribus) the price of foreign currency. When commercial actors wish to undertake any one of the three, they will contact retailing agents, who in turn place orders with firms who are wholesaling (again, this could sometimes be all within the same company). Barring offsetting demands, this will cause wholesaling inventories of the currency in question to be run down (while that of the currency be supplied by customers will rise). As they do not want to take a position in the market, this may lead those wholesaling to compensate by raising the price of the currency in demand (thus lowering that of the surplus one; this may require several hedging operations before wholesaling agents are satisfied with their exposure). Ideally, of course, wholesaling agents will have anticipated this turn of events and raised the price before the first order arrived (thus keeping the flows on both sides of the market even and reducing the necessity for covering transactions). But in either event, currency prices move. Note that this is the case even with forward contracts as wholesalers will buy the spot equivalent immediately, selling it to the customer on the day the contract matures.

What drives commercial activity and hence exchange rates? Beginning with imports, these rise as domestic national income rises (and domestic agents wish to buy more goods and services, including foreign ones) and falls as the relative price of foreign goods and services rises. Accordingly, a rise in US national income, for example, would lead to a rise in US imports and a subsequent dollar depreciation as the level of world demand for foreign currency (as compared to that for the dollar) would have risen. An increase in the relative price of foreign goods and services would do the opposite and hence cause a dollar appreciation.

There is substantial evidence, incidentally, that trade flows tend to be price inelastic but income elastic, such that large changes in exchange rates or national price indices have only a small and delayed effect on trade flows while fluctuations in overall economic activity (GDP, for example) has a quick and substantial impact (see, for example, Chinn 2005). We have had dramatic examples of large current account imbalances being very resilient in the face of substantial exchange rate depreciations over the past several decades. Imports do respond to price changes, but the impact tends to be delayed and muted.

Direct foreign investment is somewhat more complex, but a pattern emerges nevertheless. To begin, direct foreign investment can either be vertical (along the stages of production of a given product; for example, a tire manufacturer may acquire foreign rubber plantations abroad) or horizontal (at the same stage of production; for example, if that same tire manufacturer establishes another tire manufacturing plant in a different country). Horizontal direct foreign investment is often market-seeking and therefore tends to be attracted to nations with high levels of income and similar tastes to those in the source country; vertical is typically resource-seeking and moves to nations with cheap supplies of those resources (including labor) necessary to add value to the product in question. As direct foreign investment is attracted to an economy for whatever reason (e.g., a rise in domestic income attracting horizontal or a fall in domestic prices attracting vertical), so its currency appreciates and that of the source country depreciates. Hence, a rise in national income might tend to attract horizontal direct foreign investment and lead to a domestic currency appreciation, while a fall in factor costs would do the same but via vertical direct foreign investment.

As explained in Chapter One, however, as large and important as trade flows and direct foreign investment are, it is portfolio capital that dominates the market for foreign exchange. The factors driving financial flows are many but can in general be reduced at this stage to asset yield, default risk, and liquidity.[9] The greater the yield an agent expects to earn, the greater the demand for the asset; the greater the default risk, the less enthusiastic an agent is to buy; and the easier one suspects it will be to liquidate the asset, the more attractive it will be. Nations whose assets are perceived to be offering a higher yield, lower chance of default, and greater liquidity will experience appreciating currencies as agents rush to buy those assets, creating net capital inflows.

In considering the purchase of foreign assets, market participants must evaluate factors related to both the issuer of the asset in question (public or private) and those related to the currency in which the asset is denominated (relative to that used by the participant). Consider equation 3.1, showing the US dollar value of a sample portfolio of sterling denominated assets:

$$V = (\$/\pounds)*BND + (\$/\pounds)*DEP + (\$/\pounds)*P_{stk}*STK \qquad\qquad 3.1$$

where V is the total US dollar value of the portfolio, $(\$/\pounds)$ is dollars per pound sterling, BND is the sterling value of bonds held, DEP is the value of bank deposits in sterling, STK is the volume of individual stocks owned, and P_{stk} is their average price (in sterling). Note that, save any adjustments to BND and DEP that must be made to account for accumulated interest income or price adjustments caused by interest rate movements, the primary factor affecting the dollar value of the first two asset types is the rate of exchange. In addition, the relatively high volatility of $(\$/\pounds)$ (especially as the agent diversifies the group represented by STK) means that it is at least as important as P_{stk} in the last expression, and probably more so. The bottom line is that when investors are forecasting foreign asset values, *expected changes in currency prices are a key factor*. Therefore nations with currencies that are expected to appreciate will attract portfolio capital flows, causing an immediate appreciation.

To say that this is a self-fulfilling prophecy at work is true at a very basic level, but it glosses over the fact that there may be a very reasonable and well-considered rationale underlying the prophecy (as will be argued in Chapter Five in the context of the mental model). Note first that the variables upon which agents must focus in generating these foreign exchange predictions depend on which activity (imports, direct foreign investment, or portfolio foreign investment) they perceive as dominating the market. If, for example, they believed that imports constituted the majority of foreign exchange transactions, then portfolio capital investors would be well served to pay careful attention to the determinants of the sales of goods and services across national borders (i.e., national income and relative prices) and react accordingly. For instance, if portfolio investors expected a nation's income to rise, then they would come to the conclusion that the nation's imports were about to increase. As this would eventually drive down the value of the currency and thus hurt the value of assets issued by that country, market participants would immediately sell those assets. The outflow of portfolio investment would then cause the very depreciation agents feared.[10] This is a self-fulfilling prophecy, but one based on a reasonable evaluation of the circumstances. If the anticipated increase in that nation's income does not come to pass, then agents may revise their forecast and move the currency price in a different direction next period – but in the meantime, currency prices did change and economic activity was forced to adjust to the new level.

In point of fact, of course, it is portfolio investment and not trade that dominates world business, and in particular flows in search of short-term capital gain (Krause 1991, Schulmeister 1987, Shelton 1994, and Walter 1991). In that case, what agents monitor most are the determinants of portfolio foreign investment. If the flows into a particular country are expected to increase then that nation's currency can be expected to appreciate; and if its currency can be expected to appreciate, then it is safe to assume that this will, ceteris paribus, attract portfolio capital. The expected appreciation subsequently causes actual inflows of financial capital, which leads to the spot market currency appreciation that was expected.

If this is indeed the manner in which the market operates then it is apparent that determining the process by which agents form expectations is vital to explaining exchange rates. It is also important to note that the foreign exchange forecast drives *today's* rate, not the one it is forecasting. Today's expectation of next week's spot rate affects today's spot rate. Whether or not the forecast turns out to be an accurate predictor of the spot rate is an interesting question, but it is not the central one. Our concern with the forecast is a function of its role as a driver of current rates, not as an indicator of future ones.

THE CHARACTER OF EXPECTATIONS IN THE FOREIGN CURRENCY MARKET

To reiterate, since portfolio capital flows dominate the foreign exchange market it can be said that *it is today's expectations of future currency price movements that play the most important role in determining the current foreign exchange rate.* Today's prices are created by the weighted (by liquidity and confidence) average of market participants' expectations of tomorrow's price. Agents are not, as in rational expectations, forecasting an event that is independent of their actions – they are creating the event (Davidson 1982–83). Realized outcomes clearly affect the exchange rate (as, for example, importers demand foreign currency and cause the latter to appreciate), but even then the current structure of the currency market means that they do so primarily through expectations. The dollar moves more in reaction to the *announcement* of a trade imbalance than from the pressures created by the imbalance itself.

Before considering how the expectations are formed and decisions made, note that if the above characterization of the currency market is accepted then the standard Neoclassical conception of forecast bias becomes less important. In Neoclassicism, a bias is a persistent forecast error. Forecasts are not assumed to be usually or even necessarily correct; but, if economic agents are rational, then any errors must be random. This is because systematic errors, by their nature, can be identified and eliminated, something rational, profit-seeking agents would have a strong motivation to do.

In the world described by Neoclassicism, the lack of bias, so defined, is an important indicator of rationality and market efficiency, two of their core concepts. In their view, currency market participants' expectations, like those of weather forecasters, have no impact on the actual outcome. Back on June 4, what I and my colleagues *think* the euro will be worth on July 4 has no effect on what the euro is worth on July 4. And the amount by which my forecast ultimately misses the mark is not only a major factor in the value of my portfolio, but the pattern of such errors says something about me. If I (or all of us in aggregate) continually overestimate but I do not adjust my subsequent forecasts accordingly, then I am irrational. In addition, the fact that there are others who are rational and will make such adjustments means that they will drive me out of the market. Hence aggregate market expectations are bound to be rational (at least in the long run) because either all the participants are individually rational or, at the very least, that portion of the market that is irrational will be driven out of business. Note that one of the strengths of this approach is the fact that how market participants form their forecasts is irrelevant. Little time is spent pondering that question in Neoclassicism. Rather, it is the difference between the forecast (however created) and the realized value that is central, and logically so given their view of the phenomenon.

But because from the Post Keynesian perspective it is the forecast that creates the realized values, understanding the process by which the former is created is vital. Meanwhile, by the time the realized value associated with a particular forecast is known, the original forecast is irrelevant as market participants' energies are by then focused elsewhere. Imagine, for example, that it is Monday morning and a representative agent has spent most of the day making a forecast of the position of the euro by the following Monday (for sake of argument, take a forecast time horizon of one week as being the standard). She eventually decides that it will appreciate relative to the dollar, rising from $1.20 (the current spot rate) to $1.25. For simplicity, say that this is the consensus view and that she and all her colleagues worldwide have acted on this expectation. Further assume that their confidence in this forecast is absolute such that they continue buying the euro throughout the rest of the day until they collectively have driven the current price to $1.25.

Tuesday dawns for our representative agent and, barring any change in expectations, the euro price still stands at $1.25. This means that, assuming she acted before the price reached its maximum, her portfolio has increased in value (which was, of course, the whole point of the exercise). Does she now stand pat and wait to see if yesterday's forecast comes to pass, at which point she empties her inventory of euros? Of course not. She plans on holding those euros until conditions suggest that she should sell at least a portion of them (or buy more). Today, she works on her forecast for next Tuesday. In particular, she wants to know if there is any reason to believe something other than what she thought yesterday. A great deal of time and effort will be devoted to this and as the day wears on, so she will develop a new one-week forecast and alter her portfolio based upon it. The aggregate impact of her colleagues all over the world doing the same thing will move the exchange rate. On Wednesday, the process starts over again.

Come the following Monday, will she stop to compare the day's realized price with her forecast from a week earlier? Odds are she will not, for a couple of reasons. First, her day will be busy enough generating her next forecast. It is not immediately evident that there is more to be gained from analyzing the last week's events than there is from monitoring today's currency markets. If time is the ultimately scarce resource, reading the European Central Bank's latest statement (and market reactions thereto) is likely to be far more profitable than reliving the past seven days. Furthermore – and this is the more critical point – her forecast one week ago was made ceteris paribus. But everything else did not stay equal. Perhaps by today the euro really stands at $1.23 (recall that her original forecast was $1.25). This may cause no concern whatsoever on the part of our representative agent, because she may feel that intervening events fully justify this new level, rendering her original forecast moot. She is not terribly concerned with the difference between her forecast and the realized value seven days later; however, what would have caused her great consternation would have been if one week ago when the euro stood at $1.20 and she forecast it to move to $1.25 (and therefore bought euros), the euro had fallen to $1.19 by the next day. Under those circumstances, *regardless of how accurate her forecast eventually proved to be*, the fact that her expectation was out of line with that of the majority of the market on day one will be a source of considerable worry. This is Keynes' beauty contest, and it is the critical problem for the representative agent. This is why the focus in the Post Keynesian world is the difference between today's forecast of next week and today's realized price – not next week's.

There cannot be, of course, any difference between today's aggregate forecast of next week's rate and today's realized price (save that created by the lack of forecast confidence that may lead agents to hedge their bets). This is a matter of concern only to individual agents. So, a) while bias in the Neoclassical sense can still exist, it is not a theoretically significant issue, and b) there simply cannot be a "bias" gap between today's average market forecast and today's realized price.

This does not mean that there is no concept of bias in the Post Keynesian perspective, however. As will be seen below, modern psychology argues that the factors guiding decision-making may introduce of a number of varieties thereof. But in this context, "bias" does not mean forecast error; it is instead the unreasonable influence of some factor in the formation of the forecast.[11] This unreasonable influence, if widely shared, does not lead to a mistake. It instead becomes part of the realized price. It is important not because it indicates the rationality or irrationality of market participants, but because it influences the objective variable and economic activity is forced to adjust to it. Note that this bias (theoretically, if not by the agents) is known on the day of the forecast; the Neoclassical one cannot be known until the date of the object of the forecast has come. To distinguish it from the latter (hereafter referenced as realized-forecast bias), it will be called forecast-construction bias.

DECISION MAKING AND FORECASTING IN THE FOREIGN CURRENCY MARKET

Because Post Keynesian economists see agents' expectations as key determinants of foreign currency prices, explaining the latter is an essential step in building a theory of exchange rate determination. Doing so will require reference to the work not only of economists (primarily Keynes), but of psychologists as well. Considerable space will be devoted to this task as some of the concepts may be quite new to the reader. Once the basics have been described, it will be possible to explain six salient features of the foreign currency market: forecast-construction bias, price volatility, bandwagon effects, technical analysis, trading limits, and profit-taking.

Stages of decision making

How do people choose? Psychologists argue that humans "rely on a limited number of heuristic principles which reduce the complex tasks of assessing probabilities and predicting values to simpler judgmental operations" (Tversky and Kahneman 1974: 1124). These heuristics enter into the decision-making process at various stages, with the latter defined as:

1 Eventuality Analysis
2 Choice and Consequence Definition
3 Decision Weight Assignment
4 Choice
5 Post-event Assessment (Harvey 1998).

In Eventuality Analysis, the actor considers all the probable future states of the world (as related to the decision to be made). Under Choice and Consequence Definition, each possible future (from step 1) is compared with the alternatives available to the actor and the consequences of the interactions of each future and choice are contemplated. The matrix below gives an example of this process of interacting possible futures with choices.

	Euro appreciation	*Euro depreciation*
Buy euros	Profit	Loss
Sell euros	Loss	Profit

For simplicity, imagine that there are only two possible futures: euro appreciation or depreciation.[12] Further assume that the agent has only two choices available: short the euro (sell it) or go long in the euro (buy it). Each cell shows the consequence of that future combined with the choice on the vertical axis. If the agent were to buy the euro and the euro appreciated, a profit would result. If they had gone long in the euro but the euro depreciated, that leads to a loss, and so on. The agent thus compares each possible future with an available choice and forecasts the consequences.

Decision weight assignment arranges the alternatives in order of preference (based on the analyses performed in stage two and the agents' estimates of the likelihood of each outcome). In terms of the choice/consequence figure above, this means ranking the alternatives "buy euros" and "sell euros." As a first approximation, this can be seen as equivalent to calculating expected values. Continuing with the above example, if the agent in question believed that there was a 70 percent chance of euro appreciation and a 30 percent chance of euro depreciation, then one would expect the agent to rank "buy euros" first and "sell euros" second.

Stage four is the point at which the actor actually selects a course of action (basically, the one with the highest decision weight). Though this does not always occur, the decision-maker may subsequently undertake Post-event Assessment, meaning that the choice and realized consequence are reviewed in the light of what was expected.

In both stages one and two, a major part of the process is the establishment of probabilities and confidence levels. More specifically, in stage one (eventuality analysis), one must decide both what might happen over the relevant time horizon and the relative likelihoods thereof, while in stage two (choice and consequence definition) one must project likely interactions (a range of potential outcomes and the probability of each) between the currently available choices and the possible futures from stage one. In the example above, these were rather straightforward. But, if eventualities had been a range of European Central Bank policies, there is no longer a clear correspondence between outcomes and profitable portfolio decisions. The effect of new financial regulations, for example, might not be obvious and thus each cell in the choice and consequence definition table above would contain multiple items, each with its own probability. This is likely to be very complex and most of our representative agent's time will be involved in stages one and two. Note that there must also be a level of confidence associated with every forecast.

Heuristics and other tendencies

Both the probability and confidence level determination that dominate eventuality analysis and choice and consequence definition require the use of the three main heuristics of human decision-making: availability, representativeness, and anchoring. With availability, which is used to estimate frequency (in the past) or likelihood (in the future), the more available something is in memory (either through imagination or recalling past instances), the more frequent or likely that event is deemed. So, for example, because instances of snow in January are easier to recollect/imagine than instances of snow in August (in the northern hemisphere), agents will declare the former to be more likely than the latter. Such events come to mind more easily and are therefore believed to have a higher chance of occurring. Representativeness is used when one is concerned with the probability that object A belongs to class B (i.e., the chance that event A is the result of process B, or that process B will create event A). The more A resembles B, so the heuristic goes, the more likely that it belongs to class B. The series of coin tosses T-H-T-H-T may be deemed more likely the outcome of a random coin toss than T-T-T-T-H because the former better represents randomness (where the outcomes are event A and the tossing of a fairly-weighted coin is process B). Anchoring occurs when the individual must make a forecast. When this is done by starting at some initial estimate and then adjusting, people tend to anchor to that first value *regardless of the process used to generate it.*

All three of these are very useful under most circumstances, but each also introduces what I will call "forecast-construction bias." For example, availability seems on the surface to be a very reasonable approach, and one that saves computational effort. Of course it is true that snow is more likely in January, and it is not necessary to consult any meteorological charts to come to this conclusion. The inherent problem is, however, that *there are many things that can make something more available in memory without making it more frequent or likely.* An instance may be more easily accessed, for example, simply because it was dramatic, more recent, or falls into the decision maker's area of interest. The ease with which a scenario can be constructed or the search set used can also bias availability (which can be a particular issue when the agent is employing a specific mental model; phenomena that do not "fit" will be subconsciously ignored). This means that in forecasting exchange rate movements, agents may overrate the importance of events that were more recent or dramatic or fit preconceptions. These are forecast-construction biases, as opposed to realized forecast biases, and they will be reflected in currency prices.

Like availability, representativeness is both a useful heuristic that allows us to arrive at reasonable answers with a minimum of effort and a method that carries with it inherent biases. In general, the issue with representativeness is that in considering whether or not outcome A is a function of some process B (or, similarly, what outcome A will be generated by process B), agents allow for very little variation between A and B. In other words, people expect a random coin toss to look like H-T-H-T-H-T, and are tolerant of only very little deviation from the 50-50 distribution of heads and tails. If a different pattern is evident, then agents assume that there must be some distinct process at work which creates precisely that event. Thus, people expect causation where chance may be dominant (thereby ignoring very simple and presumably intuitive rules of statistical inference). For example, an outstanding performance by an athlete is seen to be a function of the athlete having been unusually skillful over that period. That the performance could be a result of a random variation from the mean is not considered.

If the law of averages is considered, representativeness means that it may be applied incorrectly. For example, agents typically expect that outliers in one direction will be offset by outliers in the other direction, even though there is no reason to suspect that tossing five heads in a row will cause the next five to display an above-average distribution of tails. That there are software programs, web sites, and books that purport to predict lottery numbers on the principle that numbers that have already been selected are less likely to be drawn a second time is attributable to representativeness. Each event is, of course, independent. Lottery numbers have no memory.

Representativeness also causes people to assume that they can make accurate predictions based on scanty information. In other words, knowing (or thinking they know) the nature of process B causes agents to believe that they can forecast outcome A. In the foreign exchange market, representativeness means that agents expect every currency movement to have a very specific cause, whether they can discern it or not. The effect of the timing of orders or other coincidences are interpreted as important market-driven trends. The willingness to forecast based on scanty information reinforces this tendency.

Anchoring puts undue weight on an individual's first estimate. Amos Tversky and Daniel Kahneman (1974) conducted a study in which individuals were asked to estimate the percentage of African countries in the United Nations. A wheel of fortune with numbers ranging from 1 to 100 was spun in front of them before they could answer, and once it had come to rest on a value, the subjects were asked to give their estimate plus or minus that value. Despite the fact that the numbers were clearly generated randomly, agents anchored their responses to them! Likewise, because the most recent time series will inform any forecast, currency market participants will tend to anchor to levels in calm markets and to rates of change in volatile ones.

Another probability-associated factor (though not a heuristic) relevant to stages one and two is that agents appear to believe that outcomes more beneficial to them are more likely.[13] This is a common psychological tendency (sometimes referenced as "wishful thinking"). Hence, one can assume that profitable outcomes will, ceteris paribus, receive a greater weight.

Through all these processes framing is also a very important issue because

> Peoples' probability judgments are not attached to events, but to descriptions of events (Tversky and Koehler 1994 and Tversky and Kahneman 1988). Events do not have likelihoods. A likelihood is an opinion, not an objective value. Opinion is based not only on the information available to the decision maker, but also on the framing of that information. Study after study has shown that the same question asked in different terms yields different answers, in stark contrast to the predictions of expected utility theory. Framing is an issue not only in the description of events, but also in the structure of the choice being made (Redelmeier and Tversky 1992). A change in either has the potential to change the decision that is made, and thus framing must be considered an important factor in the decision-making process and in probability assessment.
>
> (Harvey 1998: 54)

Events must be interpreted and agents do this within a particular social context. They share beliefs about what causes outcomes, and this mental model is a major determinant of what they interpret as relevant and how they do so (this will be discussed further in Chapter Five).

The above – availability, representativeness, anchoring, wishful thinking, and framing – all deal with the manner in which probabilities are calculated in eventuality analysis and choice and consequence definition. The specific impact of these will be outlined later in the chapter. For now, suffice it to say that in the process of collecting information, forming forecasts, and making decisions, when it is necessary to calculate a probability, agents will generally rely upon the principles inherent in the above mechanisms and their mental model. Forecast-construction bias is a natural by-product of the process; in particular, agents will place undue emphasis on dramatic and more recent events, ignore basic statistical principles, anchor to early estimates, have a tendency to expect events that favor them, and tend to ignore evidence that does not fit their preconceptions. These have specific consequences in the currency market.

Forecasts such as those formulated in stages one and two will also have confidence levels associated with them. The main principle is that the more easily the decision-maker was able to make a probability judgment based on the available information (i.e., the greater the weight of the argument), the greater the confidence in that judgment. Also, if agents are engaging in Post-Event Assessment, then any forecast errors that they discover would reduce overall confidence. Conversely, the substantiation of earlier predictions increases confidence. Note that price volatility tends, ceteris paribus, to decrease confidence.

Stage three requires the assignment of decision weights to each alternative. As suggested above, at first glance this can be viewed as equivalent to the expected values of rational choice theory. There are a number of key differences, however. First, the agent will (ceteris paribus) prefer the option in which she has more confidence. If I determine that there is a 75 percent chance of a euro appreciation and that same probability of a yen appreciation, but I have more confidence in my yen forecast, then it will receive a higher decision weight. In addition, psychologists have discovered that people prefer risky options when they feel as if they are losing and safe ones when winning (Tversky and Kahneman 1992: 298). Agents holding appreciating currencies are therefore more inclined to select options that allow them to take profits, while those with depreciating monies will want to not only avoid realizing their losses, but undertake further deals that might create offsetting revenues. Last, agents will prefer the option that is most likely to allow them to claim credit and avoid blame. For example, strong incentives exist to follow the crowd, even when (ceteris paribus) an individual believes the best course lies elsewhere. Consider the following matrix showing the choices faced by a market participant (vertical) and the possible outcomes (horizontal):

	Correct Decision	*Incorrect Decision*
With Conventional Logic	Rational	Unlucky
Against Conventional Logic	Lucky	Ignorant

The four cells cross-referencing choices and results show the manner in which the market participant's actions are likely to be interpreted (by peers, customers, supervisors, etc.). Note the incentive to move with the crowd: someone going against the majority and losing is clearly an ignorant individual, while doing so and winning is only marginally better as it may be interpreted as luck; but those choosing to move with the crowd are rewarded with a positive characterization of their choice when correct and they may receive at least a partial dispensation if incorrect.

Once decision weights are assigned, the choice stage is generally a matter of picking the alternative with the highest weight (unless agents lack sufficient confidence regarding a decision, in which case they may postpone it).

In stage five, agents *may* review past decisions with an eye toward refining one's decision-making. This can be useful, but it is often the case that the framing of decisions and means of data collection is not conducive to this process. To further compromise the matter, people tend to recall their past decisions as having been more successful than they actually were. Finally, as explained above, by the time the forecast date has arrived, agents may be focusing more energies on the next forecast than reviewing the past.

Keynes on forecasting and decision making

Keynes' insights into the workings of asset markets add to the psychological view. He makes five observations that are particularly relevant here:

1   Uncertainty – Because in general our knowledge of the future is "vague and scanty" (Keynes 1964: 148), the information of which we are aware plays a disproportionate role in our forecasts. For example, if event X depends on factors A, B, C, D, and E, but because of the nature of the world we are only able to know one piece of information at any given time (A, for example), it will play a larger role in our forecast of X than if A, B, C, D, and E were known.

2   Convention – Asset market participants adopt the convenient convention "that the existing market valuation, however arrived at, is uniquely correct in relation to our existing knowledge of the facts which will influence the yield of the investment, and that it will only change in proportion to changes in this knowledge; though philosophically speaking it cannot be uniquely correct, since our existing knowledge does not provide a sufficient basis for a calculated mathematical expectation." (Keynes 1964: 152).

3   Low Confidence – Since knowledge of the future is "vague and scanty," levels of confidence are likely to be fairly low in asset markets (though this is offset by our animal spirits; see number five below). Forecasts are therefore "… liable to change violently as the result of a sudden fluctuation of opinion" (Keynes 1964: 154).

4   Quick Results – "… human nature desires quick results, there is a particular zest in making money quickly, and remoter gains are discounted by the average man at a very high rate" (Keynes 1964: 157).

5   Animal Spirits – Humans exhibit "animal spirits," or a "spontaneous urge to action rather than inaction" (Keynes 1964: 161). This offsets any misgivings we may have about making important decisions in an uncertain world and allows us to act despite our ignorance.[14]

These will be melded into the psychological view in the analyses that follow.

SALIENT MARKET CHARACTERISTICS

Orthodox economics has struggled not just to explain overall currency price determination, but to account for commonly observed phenomena like bandwagons and bias. Explanations that do exist tend to be inconsistent with parallel explanations in the same source (a common situation in textbooks) or relegated to the short run and, therefore, white-noise status. By contrast, the combination of the psychological view and Keynes' observations offered here yields a description of a decision-making process that includes inherent forecast-construction biases, tends to create price volatility and bandwagons, and leads agents to employ technical analysis, take risks, and engage in periodic profit taking.

Forecast construction bias

That the first is true should be clear from the psychology. As has already been explained, persistent forecast-construction biases are associated with availability, representativeness, anchoring, and the tendency to expect favorable events and ignore those that do not fit preconceptions. These biases are incorporated into the price and thus those who try to "avoid" them do so at their own risk. Forecasting the psychology of market means treating these as important determinants and not errors.

Volatility

With respect to volatility, there is no question that it has been so great that it cannot be explained by changes in underlying "fundamentals" (Quinn and Harvey 1998). The Post Keynesian approach blames the volatility on the manner in which agents' forecasts are formed. It is created by uncertainty, availability, representativeness, anchoring, the desire for quick results, animal spirits, and convention. Uncertainty means that as events emerge, so agents, lacking the whole picture, are likely to give them disproportionate weight and react accordingly. Representativeness works to reinforce this as it encourages people to think that they can and should make forecasts based on small samples. If the event that created the initial price movement was particularly dramatic then the availability heuristic leads agents to overweight it in their forecast; and once volatility starts, anchoring may exacerbate it as attention shifts from price levels to price changes (in other words, agents anchor forecasts to the changes such that they begin to expect them rather than stability). Throughout this process, agents' desire for quick results and the willingness to act even when lacking a firm basis for decision making (i.e., animal spirits) makes the emergence of sudden and violent price movements, if not a daily event, certainly not surprising. One might think that convention – the belief that today's price is uniquely correct given our knowledge of all that has transpired up to this moment

– would encourage stability. It may under some circumstances. However, it also means that each time some new event occurs, agents feel bound to assume that further prices changes are inevitably warranted. This may occur even when the "new" information is simply the continuation of an existing state of affairs (an interest-rate differential, for example).

Volatility feeds on volatility, but only to an extent. If it becomes too great, agents' increasing lack of confidence (which is likely as prices become unstable) may eventually win over, causing them to withdraw from the market (closing out their positions). Calm will then be restored, until events conspire to create a new period of volatility.[15]

Bandwagons

A bandwagon occurs when a price moves in a particular direction only because it has done so earlier. Agents "jump on the bandwagon" by purchasing the appreciating asset or selling the depreciating one, having no more justification than "everyone else seems to be doing it." Bandwagons are another controversial phenomenon in financial markets that can be explained by reference to the Post Keynesian view of forecast determination. They can be seen as a result of availability, anchoring, representativeness, increasing confidence (created by forecast substantiation), and credit/blame issues. As a price movement begins, it is a salient event and therefore more available in memory. Thus, because of the availability heuristic, it plays a disproportionate role in market participants' forecast – particularly if it was dramatic. Agents may also be expected to anchor to that movement (rather than the level), contributing to the emerging trend as they begin to expect change rather than stability. Representativeness convinces agents that there must be some reason for the movement (if event A is occurring then there must surely be some process B behind it) even if they, individually, do not understand it. Hence, market participants assume that they should be taking the positions implied by the recent price changes. Then, as the price continues in the same direction, those forecasting the movement (the numbers of whom may be increasing) will be encouraged by the apparent substantiation of their predictions and thus become increasingly confident and willing to commit funds. Finally, those ignoring the bandwagon run the risk of being thought foolish, while those jumping on it only to have it go bust can fall back on the excuse, "But everyone else was doing it!" Bandwagons will continue until events (as interpreted by the market participants) indicate otherwise. If those events are sufficiently out of sync with the current run then the confidence of agents may be shattered and a collapse and panic may result.[16]

Technical analysis

Technical analysis amounts to manipulations of past time series of the currency price in order to predict future movements. For example, one may compare a long-term moving average (e.g., the average closing price for the past ten days) with a short-term one (e.g., the average closing price for the past three days).

The typical rule is that if the short-term average passes above the long-term, buy the currency in question (and vice versa). Neoclassical economics argues that reliance on such a tool is futile since past price movements are available to everyone. If they contained valuable information then the market would already reflect this. However, Mark Taylor and Helen Allen (1992) found that technical trading rules were very widely used in the foreign currency market. Why would such a simple method be employed by so many professionals if it did not generate profit? From the Post Keynesian perspective the answer is simple: trading rules are profitable, and it is because bandwagon effects make them so. Bear in mind that technical analysis is almost invariably based on the premise that emerging trends will continue (Rosenberg 1996: 324). Any of the various techniques – moving average, momentum, or point and figure, for example – gives a buy signal if recent prices are higher than past ones and a sell if recent prices are lower than past ones (Schulmeister 1988). If prices continue their climb or fall, then such a rule will result in profit. And if a bandwagon is at work, that is exactly what will happen. Hence, trading rules do not need to rely on self-fulfilling prophecy (as some have argued); they simply take advantage of the fact that bandwagons exist. Technical analysis predicts a trend and the bandwagon effect obliges by creating it.

Trading limits and cash in

Another factor that can be explained with the above tools is the existence of trading limits in currency rooms. It is a very common practice to restrict the open positions currency dealers may maintain and to set limits on the losses they can incur before they are required to close them out (Weisweiller 1991 and Hudson 1979). This is done because of peoples' psychological attitude toward risk, outlined above. When agents feel they are in a losing situation they will tend to choose more risky options, to "let it ride" and hope that the falling asset price, for example, will turn around at some point. This reluctance to realize a loss can get a trading room into a great deal of trouble, as Barings Bank found out with Nick Leeson in 1995 (Cornford 1996). Hence, limits are placed on dealers so they will not have a choice.[17]

The flip side of this is agents' attitude when winning. Under these circumstances, they tend to become risk averse. This is why we observe cash in or profit taking. As a currency appreciates, those holding it become increasingly anxious about realizing what have been up to now only paper profits. Hence, we observe the whipsaw pattern described by Schulmeister (1987, 1988) wherein even a steadily rising foreign exchange value is continually interrupted by short drops (the moments at which agents cash in).[18]

Mental model

One last factor to be introduced (but not fully developed until Chapter Five) is the mental model. As suggested in the discussion of framing, the preconceptions of agents are terribly important both in terms of what they consider to be useful inputs into the forecasting and decision making process and in how they believe those inputs will ultimately affect currency prices. These preconceptions, which comprise the mental model, are a social product. Currency market participants are members of a particular subculture. What they believe about how the world works is a direct function of the views of their educators, colleagues, family, friends, kin, et cetera. They seek out the advice of experts, they read professional and scholarly literature, and they consciously and subconsciously mimic the behavior of various role models. We cannot understand the foreign exchange market without understanding what these participants themselves think they are doing.

CONCLUSIONS

This chapter starts the process of developing the tools necessary to understand the foreign currency market. It is argued that portfolio capital flows dominate the market and that within that context market participants' forecasts of future currency price movements are the prime movers of foreign exchange rates. The offered model of expectations and decision making (based on psychological research and the economics of Keynes) suggests that the market will swing between periods of calm and volatility, that bandwagon effects will be prevalent, and that the foci of expectations formation will emerge as a function of the social context in which the agents interpret their experiences and scholars and professionals engage in research. Once the relationship between exchange rates and the balance of payments is outlined in the next chapter, the following one will use the insights gained to develop a Post Keynesian model of currency price determination.

4 Leakages, injections, exchange rates, and trade (im)balances

Recall from Chapter One that the Neoclassical version of macroeconomics assumes an automatic tendency toward full employment. In the example offered there, whenever a decline in investment threatened to lower the level of aggregate demand, the rate of interest would fall sufficiently to reinvigorate spending and stave off recession. In the absence of frictions or other impediments to the free-market process, the rate of interest acts to maintain the level of demand necessary for full employment to prevail.

The larger story here is one of leakages and injections. Leakages from the income stream (like saving) lower the level of aggregate demand, while injections (like investment) increase it. In equilibrium, leakages must equal injections, but it is the route by which they arrive at that point that determines the character of the macroeconomy as that equilibrium may or may not be consistent with the full-employment level of output. As suggested above, in the Neoclassical story, spending is able to remain at that maximum while interest rate adjustments set leakages equal to injections; in the Post Keynesian story, however, it is the level of economic activity that bears the burden. This means that it is entirely possible, even probable, that economic activity could come to rest at the less-than-full employment level in seeking a position consistent with the leakages-injections equilibrium.

Consider these opposing viewpoints in an open economy. If imports are added to the list of leakages and exports to the list of injections, there now exists a potential problem for Neoclassicism. While interest rates are assumed to adjust to keep savings and investment at the full employment level, they have no direct effect on imports and exports. Thus, in the absence of an alternative explanation, it is possible that a fall in exports or a rise in imports could leave the economy at a less-than-full employment equilibrium. That this does not occur is due to the fact that Neoclassical economists envision exchange rates as playing the same role in creating import/export adjustments as the interest rate does in the savings/investment sphere. Whenever net exports become negative, thus threatening the economy with recession, currency prices are expected to fall and thereby encourage exports and discourage imports. Currency depreciation reinvigorates domestic demand in the same way as an interest rate decline and it allows the economy to remain at full employment.[1]

That currency prices move so as to equalize imports and exports is a common theme in mainstream models. Ronald MacDonald writes, "… most theoretical models of exchange rate determination would define a true long-run equilibrium as one in which the current account equals zero" (MacDonald 1995: 482). And though it is rarely portrayed as such, it is one of the legs by which the full-employment assumption is maintained. However, the conditions necessary to create the automatic adjustment of exchange rates described above are very specific and, unfortunately, not descriptive of the world in which we actually live. To under-stand why this is so requires looking at the currency market in the context of the balance of payments. In the end, it will be demonstrated that when international transactions are dominated by capital and not trade flows, exchange rates do not operate to drive the latter to zero (and thereby maintain aggregate demand). Trade imbalances can continue indefinitely and, for deficit countries, they represent a drain on the level of economic activity no different than that created by a rise in savings or a fall in investment. This argument is consistent with that made by Tony Thirlwall in his balance-of-payments growth constraint theory (Arestis, McCombie, and Vickerman 2007).

EXCHANGE RATES AND THE BALANCE OF PAYMENTS

At the simplest level, there are only three reasons for demanding foreign currency:

1 importation of goods and services;
2 direct foreign investment, or purchases of foreign assets for ownership purposes; and,
3 portfolio foreign investment, or purchases of foreign assets for short-term capital gain.[2]

The total demand for any currency is simply the summation of these three. For example (taking the US as the home country and assuming for simplicity that only Americans hold dollars), the total demand for foreign currency is found by adding 1) the schedule (at various exchange rates) of foreign currency desired by US agents who wish to purchase foreign goods and services, 2) the schedule of foreign currency desired by US agents who wish to purchase foreign assets for ownership purposes, and 3) the schedule of foreign currency desired by US agents who wish to purchase foreign assets for short-term capital gain.

Figure 4.1 offers a graphic illustration of the demand for foreign currency for the dollar-foreign currency ($-FX) market. The presentation is very simple, with E as the price of foreign currency in dollars ($/FX), Q of FX the quantity of foreign currency, and D for FX the demand for foreign currency as derived from the demand for imports, direct foreign investment, and portfolio foreign investment. Note the negative slope implying that, ceteris paribus, the quantity of foreign currency demanded will fall as its price rises.

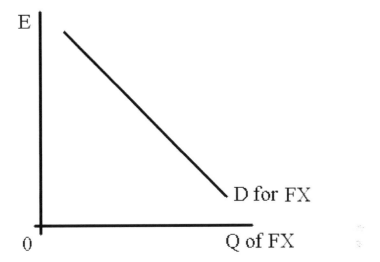

Figure 4.1 Demand for foreign currency (E = $/FX).

Figure 4.2 shows the supply of FX. Foreign currency is offered to Americans when foreigners wish to obtain dollars (its positive slope is a function of the fact that E is the inverse of the price of dollars).[3] Note that in a two-country world (or when treating the rest of the world as a single state, as here), S of FX is identical to D for $. In other words, those who are supplying foreign currency to the market are simultaneously demanding dollars (and those who are supplying dollars are demanding foreign currency). Hence, the positively sloped line in Figure 4.2 can be labeled either S of FX or D for $. We will adopt the latter as it will make the exposition more straightforward.[4] Figure 4.3 shows equilibrium in the $-FX market.

So far this tells us relatively little that is novel about the market for currency. As would be true in any market, a rise in the demand for the product (FX) will cause a rise in its equilibrium price and quantity; and a rise in supply depresses price and raises quantity. However, there is more occurring than first appears. To see this requires that we break the demand for the currencies into distinct market segments. The key is to separate currency demands derived from goods and services trade (imports and exports) from that derived from capital flows (direct foreign investment and portfolio foreign investment). Under this scheme, the total demand for foreign currency would be equal to those demanded in order to purchase foreign goods and services plus those demanded to purchase foreign assets (for both ownership and capital gain). This can be expressed,

$$\text{D for FX} = \text{D for FX } (M_{us}+K^{\circ}_{us}) = \text{D for FX } (M_{us}) + \text{D for FX } (K^{\circ}_{us}) \qquad 4.1$$

where D for FX (M_{us}) is US import demand (i.e., US demand for foreign goods and services) and D for FX (K°_{us}) is US capital outflow (i.e., US demand for foreign

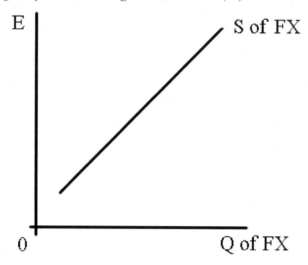

Figure 4.2 Supply of foreign currency or the demand for dollars (E = $/FX).

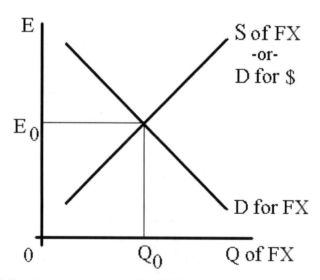

Figure 4.3 Complete currency market (E = $/FX).

assets). Equation 4.2 shows the other side of the market (recall that D for $ = S for FX):

$$\text{D for } \$ = \text{D for } \$ \ (X_{us} + K^i_{us}) = \text{D for } \$ \ (X_{us}) + \text{D for } \$ \ (K^i_{us}) \qquad 4.2$$

where D for $ (X_{us}) is US export demand (i.e., foreign demand for US goods and services) and D for $ (K^i_{us}) is US capital inflow demand (i.e., foreign demand for US assets).

Equation 4.1 is represented in Figure 4.4. The outermost function is the total demand for foreign currency: ($M_{us}+K^o_{us}$). The innermost represents only the foreign currency desired by US citizens to purchase foreign goods and services: (M_{us}). It is not necessary to illustrate D for FX (K^o_{us}) separately as it is simply the difference between D for FX ($M_{us}+K^o_{us}$) and D for FX (M_{us}) (in fact, the reason that the rightmost function is flatter than the leftmost is because the negative slope of D for FX (K^o_{us}) has been added to it). If the exchange rate were E_0, the total quantity of FX demanded would be Q_1, the quantity demanded by US importers wishing purchase foreign goods and services would be Q_0, and the quantity demanded by US investors wishing purchase foreign capital assets (direct and indirect foreign investment) would be $Q_1 - Q_0$.

This same decomposition can be done for the D for $ as well, and then combined with what is shown on Figure 4.4 to illustrate a number of interesting facts regarding exchange rates and the balance of payments. In Figure 4.5, D for $ ($X_{us}+K^i_{us}$) and D for $ (X_{us}) show the total demand for dollars by foreigners and the demand for dollars by foreigners wishing to purchase US goods and services (with the D for $ (K^i_{us}) as the difference between the two). The intersection of the curves representing the total demands for foreign currency and for dollars – D for FX ($M_{us}+K^o_{us}$) and D for $ ($X_{us}+K^i_{us}$) – shows the equilibrium exchange rate. Calculating the various components of the balance of payments is now a matter of cross referencing the equilibrium exchange rate with the various demand functions. US imports, for example, are found by determining where E_0 crosses D for FX (M_{us}): Q_0. US capital outflows are found by taking the difference between D for FX ($M_{us}+K^o_{us}$) and D for FX (M_{us}) at the prevailing exchange rate. This yields $Q_1 - Q_0$. Following the same logic, US exports are Q_0 and US capital inflows are $Q_1 - Q_0$. Notice that in this instance we have balanced trade (and, of course, a balanced capital account).

Figure 4.6 gives a more interesting situation, one in which trade is imbalanced. Note first the exchange rate labeled BTER, or balanced trade exchange rate. As

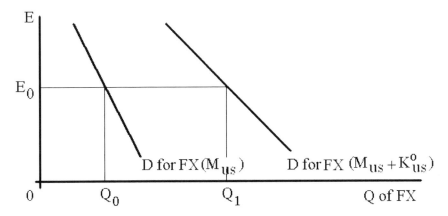

Figure 4.4 Demand for foreign currency decomposed (E = $/FX).

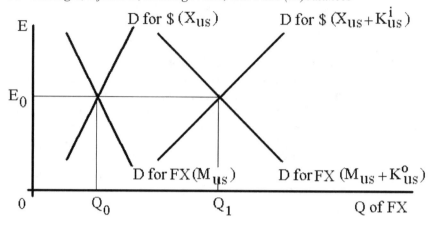

Figure 4.5 Complete market, balanced trade (E = $/FX).

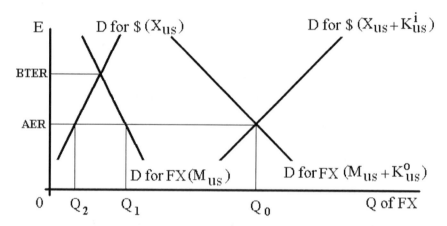

Figure 4.6 Complete market, US trade deficit and capital account surplus (E = $/FX).

the label suggests, this shows the price of FX at which trade between the US and its trading partners would be balanced. At prices higher than this, the US would enjoy a trade surplus; at prices lower, a trade deficit. The intersection of the two curves representing the total demands for currency, D for $ ($X_{us}+K^i_{us}$) and D for FX ($M_{us}+K^o_{us}$), gives the actual exchange rate, AER. As this is the price at which all transactions actually take place, US exports, imports, capital inflows, and capital outflows are calculated at that rate. US exports in Figure 4.6 (found at the intersection of D for $ (X_{us}) and AER) are Q_2 and US imports (the intersection of D for $ (M_{us}) and AER) are Q_1; US capital inflows (the difference between D for $ ($X_{us}+K^i_{us}$) and D for $ (X_{us}) at AER) will be ($Q_0 - Q_2$), while US capital outflows (the difference between D for FX ($M_{us}+K^o_{us}$) and D for FX (M_{us}) at AER) are ($Q_0 - Q_1$). Note that just as one would expect with BTER price of foreign currency exceeding actual, AER, the US has a trade deficit. Note further that this graphical approach shows very clearly the fact that the trade and capital account imbalances must be of the same size (though opposite sign) as each is represented by the identical line segment $(Q_1 - Q_2)$.

This simple framework gives insight into the effect of the composition of foreign currency demand on the balance of payments and on the role (or lack thereof) of currency prices in supporting full employment. First off, it is clear that, on the surface of it, there is no obvious reason to assume that trade imbalances self correct. For such a tendency to exist, it would be necessary for AER to be automatically attracted to the level represented by BTER. In the extreme case, if no capital flows existed then D for $ (X_{us}) and D for FX (M_{us}) would comprise the total demand for currency and thus AER would *always* be equal to BTER. This is, as argued in Chapter Two, basically what Neoclassical economics assumes (at least over the long run). In the absence of capital flows, exchange rates are a function of trade balances and they will, indeed, adjust so that those balances come to rest at zero. In this way, a nation whose economic prosperity is threatened by a current account deficit is rescued.

By extension, a world in which capital flows are very small compared to trade flows may also tend to produce something close to balanced trade. Figure 4.7 illustrates such a situation. If the sizes of D for FX (K^o_{us}) and D for $ (K^i_{us}) are limited to being no larger than shown in Figure 4.7, then AER and BTER can never stray far apart. Were the demand for US capital assets to collapse to zero (and that for foreign ones be unchanged), AER would move to point A and create a trade surplus for the US (the size of which would correspond to the horizontal line segment between D for $ (X_{us}) and D for FX (M_{us}) and across from point A). In the event that the demand for foreign capital assets fell to zero (and demand for US stayed unchanged), AER would move to point B and create a trade deficit for the US (the size of which would correspond to the horizontal line segment between

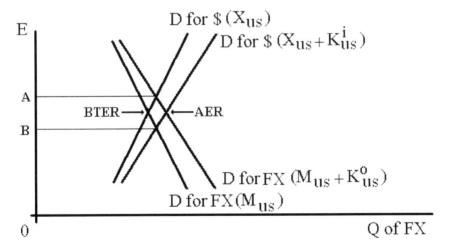

Figure 4.7 The case of small capital flows (E = $/FX).

D for $ (X_{us}) and D for FX (M_{us}) and across from point B). In any case, AER can never stray any further away from BTER than A or B; furthermore, the smaller one assumes capital flows to be, the closer A and B must be to BTER. Note further that this would create a strong incentive for those undertaking portfolio investments to pay close attention to factors driving trade flows and adjust their portfolios (and hence move the price of currency) accordingly.

As capital flows grow larger and larger, however, AER and BTER may settle further apart. Figure 4.8, for example, shows a situation in which capital flows dominate exchange rate determination (at the AER shown, capital flows are roughly four times the size of trade flows – ten times would be closer to reality). Though the figure shows the two currency prices directly across from one another, this clearly need not be the case. Capital flows here are so large that the points that would correspond to A and B in Figure 4.7 are out of view. Imbalances can be quite large when capital flows predominate, and there is little reason for portfolio capital investors to care about factors driving imports and exports. Trade is imbalanced in equilibrium and only by coincidence would it be otherwise. This is not unlike the structure of today's currency market, and under these circumstances exchange rates do not automatically act to generate sufficient demand to maintain full employment.

EXCHANGE RATES AND THE BALANCE-OF-PAYMENTS CONSTRAINT

All this is consistent with arguments made under Thirlwall's Law, or Balance-of-Payments-Constrained Growth (see for example Arestis, McCombie, and Vickerman 2007). Their central argument is that, just as a domestic macroeconomy must maintain a particular level of investment to offset savings if they are to achieve full employment, so must they achieve a particular balance of payments. A key assumption of Thirlwall's Law is that balanced trade will not automatically prevail because "the rate of exchange is ineffective in determining the growth of exports and imports," just as described earlier (McCombie 2003: 16). Extensive

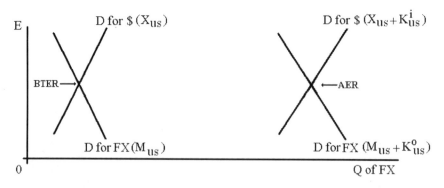

Figure 4.8 The case of large capital flows (E = $/FX).

empirical research has lent strong support to Thirlwall's contention that the balance-of-payments constraint is real and significant, particularly in developing nations (McCombie 2003).

The more important driving force behind trade flows, according to Thirlwall's Law supporters, is that set of variables comprising the non-price factors affecting imports and exports. They further fear that if a nation experiences long periods during which they are forced to finance a trade imbalance with short-term capital inflows, this will ultimately lead to a "collapse in the exchange rate and the risk of a resulting depreciation/inflation spiral" (McCombie 2003: 15). Such a scenario is easily illustrated using the framework developed in this chapter.

Figure 4.9 takes Mexico as a small, developing nation, and substitutes pesos for dollars on the graph. Note the very steep D for peso (X_{mx}), representing extreme price inelasticity for Mexican goods and services. D for FX (M_{mx}) is likewise very steep for the same reasons, but assumed to lie to the right of D for peso (X_{mx}) at all levels of peso/FX shown. The latter is based on the assumption that the world demand for goods and services produced in Mexico is rather limited, while Mexico is dependent on the rest of the world for some set of imported products (perhaps manufactured goods, technology, food, or essential minerals). Important here is the fact that no matter how cheap the peso gets, the rest of the world has a finite interest in Mexican products. There is therefore a limit in terms to how large X_{mx} can be in the short run. Meanwhile, if economic crisis is to be avoided, critically important imports (for which there is no domestic substitute) must continue to flow into Mexico.[5]

The starting points on Figure 4.9 are the far right D for peso ($X_{mx}+K^i_{mx}$) and the innermost D for peso (X_{mx}) and D for FX (M_{mx}). As drawn, the BTER is out of range of realistically achievable exchange rates. It does not matter where D for peso ($X_{mx}+K^i_{mx}$) and D for FX ($M_{mx}+K^o_{mx}$) are placed, Mexico will experience a trade deficit of largely the same size. The only factors that have a noticeable impact on the trade balance would be shifts in D for peso (X_{mx}) and D for FX (M_{mx}).

Now notice what will happen as the rising level of short-term debt in Mexico causes agents to begin to shy away from Mexican financial assets: D for peso

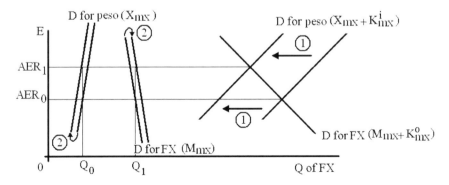

Figure 4.9 Balance-of-payments growth constraint and the depreciation/inflation spiral (E = peso/FX).

$(X_{mx}+K^i_{mx})$ will shift left because K^i_{mx} falls (shown as ①). This creates a peso depreciation and a movement of AER towards the currently unobservable BTER (there might also be a rise in K^o_{mx} as domestic agents shift their money to more secure accounts; this would magnify the depreciation). As the peso depreciates, the peso-price of the vital imports rises and domestic inflation is thereby fueled. The rise in the Mexican price level can then be expected to shift D for FX (M_{mx}) to the right and D for peso (X_{mx}) to the left (shown as ②), leaving the trade deficit largely unaffected, meaning that debt may continue to accumulate and another round of depreciation can be expected. This is the depreciation/inflation spiral predicted by Thirlwall and it shows that even when exchange rates do fall in response to a trade deficit, this does not guarantee a reduction in the current account imbalance.

CONCLUSIONS

There is no reason to believe that there is any automatic tendency for AER to be attracted to BTER. In a market where exchange rates are dominated by portfolio capital flows, only if agents' forecasting efforts focused on national trade balances would there be a tangible link between AER and BTER. For example, if market participants believed that nations with trade deficits represented greater default risks than those without, then the financial assets of such economies might become less popular among portfolio investors and the deficit nations' currencies would depreciate. This may bring AER closer to BTER, so long as a depreciation/inflation spiral is not triggered.

But surely, one might interject, a nation cannot accumulate debt indefinitely? There is no question that it creates a burden and that under some circumstances a limiting point may be reached. But, it is possible to carry even increasing levels of debt for a very long time. Anwar Shaikh has argued that a common state of affairs is for the deficit nation to be offered special financing or a chance to refinance (Shaikh 1980 and 1996 and Shaikh and Antonopoulos 1998). If this is true and private investors are not ignorant of this, it is yet another means by which the link between AER and BTER is weakened.

Meanwhile, the impact of trade balances on currency forecasts is already dampened among large, developed economies. While one can identify periods during which deficit nations experienced sustained depreciations (take for example the market's focus on trade balances immediately following the collapse of Bretton Woods), these have been the exception rather than the rule. These periods have occurred and we should not ignore them, but nor should we imagine that trade flows play the central role assumed by Neoclassical approaches. The simple fact is that the determinants of the market for foreign goods and services (driving BTER) are distinct from those determining the demand for foreign assets (which, for all intents and purposes, drives AER). There is no reason we should expect one price to clear two markets. When there has been a link, it has been because portfolio investors have decided that there should be. In general, portfolio capital flows determine exchange rates.

5 Post Keynesian exchange rate modeling

This chapter presents a formal Post Keynesian analysis of exchange rate determination. It begins with a review of what was learned in the earlier chapters and then moves on to a full-scale, open-economy macro model and a graphical depiction of agents' mental model and the expectation-formation process.

EXCHANGE RATE DETERMINATION THUS FAR

The last two chapters introduced concepts ranging from psychology to balance of payments accounting. The ultimate aim of those discussions was the illumination of the process of exchange rate determination. The following points were made:

1 *There is no reason to expect exchange rates to move in a way that restores balanced trade.* That exchange rates do just that is a central theme in almost every Neoclassical theory (MacDonald 1995: 482). This is an offshoot of their discounting of the role of portfolio capital and it is a leg of their argument that the economy tends toward full employment. But if uncertainty is assumed and financial flows are allowed a significant role, there is absolutely no reason to expect the actual exchange rate to be drawn to the level that would eliminate trade imbalances. Even if market participants believe that nations with trade deficits are, for example, default risks, leading them to sell that nation's currency and hence reduce the imbalance by causing the currency to depreciate, this is neither inevitable nor will it likely be sufficient. Furthermore, if it does occur, it is a function of a change in expectations in the financial capital market rather than of events in the market for goods and services.

2 *A combination of psychological theory and Keynes' insights into asset markets suggests that currency prices go through cycles of volatility.* This is a function of uncertainty, availability, representativeness, anchoring, the desire for quick results, animal spirits, and convention. Volatility feeds on itself as agents' anchor for forecasts shifts from levels to changes; but, if it grows too large, the increasing lack of confidence on the part of market participants will cause them to close out positions and withdraw from the market, restoring calm.

3 *Bandwagon effects exist because of availability, anchoring, representativeness,*

increasing confidence, and credit/blame issues. These can continue unabated until current events (as interpreted by market participants) accumulate against the trend. If the discrepancy between the level to which a currency price has risen due to bandwagons and the interpretation of events is large enough then agents' confidence can be shattered and panic and collapse can result.

4   *It is because bandwagons exist that technical analysis is useful/profitable.* Trading rules are based on the premise that emerging trends will continue; bandwagons *cause* emerging trends to continue.

5   *People's attitude toward risk creates the whipsaw pattern Schulmeister (1987, 1988) describes.* As a held currency rises in value, so the anxiety created by the possibility that it might reverse (hence destroying paper profits) increases. Therefore, a sustained appreciation will be interrupted by frequent profit taking (or cash in). Such is the level of that anxiety that in the floating period, sustained (daily) appreciations or depreciations have lasted no more than two days three-quarters of the time, and less than four days in 90 percent of all cases (author's calculations of the post-Bretton Woods dollar-Deutsche mark and dollar-euro).

6   *Psychological theory shows that expectations and decisions naturally include forecast-construction bias.* Some factors may exert an unreasonable influence on the expectation-formation process. But because everyone shares it, this bias is not an "error" and is thus not punished and thereby eliminated.

7   *How confident agents are in their forecast is a critical issue that cannot be ignored.* It affects both the level at which the exchange rate comes to rest and the volatility and stability of the market. It is also a major reason that uncovered interest rate parity does not hold, as will be explained later in this chapter.

While all these add something interesting and useful to our quest to understand exchange rates, even in combination they still fall short of an operational model of currency-price determination. They can serve as inputs and guideposts, but not as ends in themselves. This chapter fills this void by introducing an open-economy Z-D diagram, a model of agents expectations, and a model of financial crises. The first illustrates the relationships among the currency market, domestic macroeconomy, and international balances. It employs Keynes' Z-D diagram and endogenous money and in it the currency market is driven by portfolio capital flows. There is no assumption of a tendency toward full employment or balanced trade and the central role of income effects in driving trade flows and the importance of financial factors in determining exchange rates will be highlighted. The expectations model offers a concrete specification of agents' forecasting and decision making, but one sufficiently flexible to allow for unique historical events and the evolution of agents' worldview. It shows how bandwagon effects manifest themselves and which inputs tend to play the core role. The model of financial crises combines the lessons of the expectations model with Minky's Financial Instability Hypothesis. It will be shown that crises are a matter of course in capitalist economies, but that the specific manner in which they manifest themselves may vary. Note that while all three models are assumed to apply to either developed or developing nations, it is likely that the first two (the open-economy Z-D and the expectations-formation schematic) will find more applications in advanced, industrial economies while the last (the crisis model) may be most useful in understanding non-industrialized countries.

OPEN-ECONOMY Z-D DIAGRAM

Recall that the Dornbusch model consisted of four markets: IS-LM, uncovered interest rate parity, purchasing power parity, and a Monetarist-style aggregate supply-aggregate demand model (see Figure 2.5). Each was linked to another market via one of its axes. The same general method will be applied here.

The macro portion of this model will be represented by Keynes' Z-D diagram (see Figure 5.1).[1] This was originally laid out in Chapter Three of the *General Theory*, "The Principle of Effective Demand." It is written in (N_{us}, Py_{us}) space,

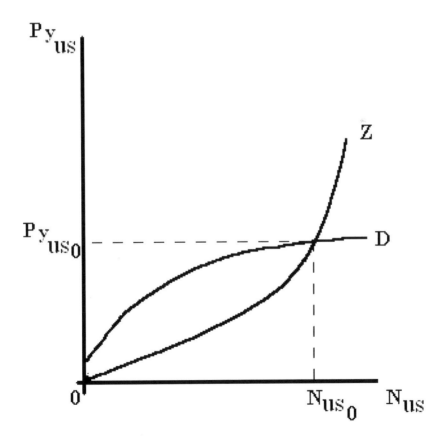

Figure 5.1 Keynes' Z-D diagram.

where (taking for convenience the United States as the home country) N_{us} is US employment and Py_{us} is nominal GDP in the US. Note first that describing economic activity in nominal terms stands in stark contrast to the standard approach. Keynes insisted that this was more appropriate since firms sell for and consumers buy at *money* prices. The deflators we use to create real values are, while perhaps useful for historical studies, of limited relevance in considering the short-term behavior of macroeconomic agents. Economists may use real values, but firms and consumers do not.[2]

Returning to the specification of the model, the D curve represents the nominal sales generated when N workers are employed and is called the "*Aggregate Demand Function*" (Keynes 1964: 25). The slope is a result of the consumption function and relies on the assumption that as income rises from the employment of more workers, so does consumption (measured on Py), but at a declining rate. Hence the positive but diminishing slope. The vertical intercept depends on non-consumption aggregate demand (in other words, spending that is not a direct function of N). In the *General Theory*, this meant investment, though one could easily add other types such as net government spending and net exports. This can be expressed as

$$D = I + C \qquad\qquad 5.1$$

where D is aggregate demand, I is nominal investment spending, and C is nominal consumption spending. While I is exogenous, C is, as explained above, a function of current employment:

$$C = F(N) \atop + \qquad\qquad 5.2$$

The Z curve is the "aggregate supply price of the output from employing N men" (Keynes 1964: 25), or the revenue that firms must expect to earn before they are willing to hire a given number of workers. It is simply the standard orthodox profit maximizing condition in a perfectly competitive market (marginal cost = marginal revenue) written in (N,Py) space:

$$Z = N(W*apn/mpn) \qquad\qquad 5.3$$

where N is defined as above, W is the nominal wage, apn is the average product of labor, and mpn is the marginal product of labor.[3] Taking a point on the horizontal axis, the corresponding Py given by Z is the level of sales that entrepreneurs must expect if they are to hire that N (i.e. Py is the level of sales that would maximize profits given the aggregate demand generated by the employment of N workers). Z becomes steeper because of the fact that there are diminishing marginal returns as workers are added to fixed capital. Each worker must be paid the same wage, but additional ones produce less and less output. Sales must therefore increase at an increasing rate if more employees are to be profitably added to the payroll.

Taking Z and D together, their intersection is Keynes' point of "*effective demand*" (Keynes 1964: 25):

$$I + C = N(W*apn/mpn) \qquad 5.4$$

Anywhere to the right, and the resulting point on Z would lie above the corresponding point on D. As the former yields the Py firms need to be satisfied with the current level of employment but the latter is what will actually prevail, entrepreneurs will be disappointed and lay off workers (moving us back to the left). Meanwhile, if firms choose an N to the left of the point of effective demand, this leaves them facing an excess demand for their products; they will adjust next period by hiring more workers (moving N to the right). Note that a key feature of the Z-D diagram is that there is no expectation that the level of employment that prevails is the one associated with full employment (the latter can be indicated on the horizontal axis, but it is a reference point only and plays no role in the determination of equilibrium). In fact, ceteris paribus, the decreasing slope of D and the increasing slope of Z combine to frustrate the goal of achieving higher levels of employment since it means that fewer and fewer sales will result from higher employment, while achieving the latter requires just the opposite, i.e. higher and higher sales. The economy can come to rest at less-than-full employment indefinitely.[4]

A number of things can change the slope and position of Z and D. For example, beginning with the former, a rise in nominal wages will shift the curve inward (with the intercept remaining at the origin) as firms hire fewer workers at each level of nominal sales because of the higher wage bill. If productivity rises, Z shifts right since firms require lower levels of Py to maximize profits given the higher levels of output produced by each N. With respect to demand, a change in income distribution toward the wealthy would flatten D (as it would yield lower levels of consumption at each N), while a rise in any non-consumption spending – government expenditures, investment, or net exports – will cause an upward shift.

Expanding on the factors that can cause a shift, government spending will be treated as exogenous, but investment (I) is a function of interest rates (r_{us}) and the expected rate of profit from investment (π^e):

$$I = (r_{us}, \pi^e) \qquad 5.5$$
$$-\phantom{r_{us},}+$$

As usual, it is assumed that as interest rates rise, this causes the cost of financing investment to increase and thus the rate of capital formation to decline; and as firms expect a greater rate of profit from investment, so they engage in more. It is further assumed, along general Post Keynesian lines, that the impact of changes in π^e is far greater than that of changes in r_{us}. That is to say, it would not be improbable to see high levels of investment alongside high interest rates or low levels with low rates, but one would almost never witness high levels of capital formation when π^e is low or low levels when π^e is high, regardless of interest rates.

This leaves net exports as the last unexplained factor that may shift D. It is specifically modeled in the diagram. The current account is illustrated in Figure 5.2. The horizontal axis shows the exchange rate while the vertical is nominal income. BTFX is the locus of points showing the combinations of Py_{us} and the exchange rate, E (measured as \$/FX), that would yield balanced trade for the US. As such, for every level of domestic nominal income it shows the exchange rate that would have to prevail (*ceteris paribus*) to make exports exactly equal to imports (this was described as the balanced trade exchange rate, or BTER, in the FX/BOP diagram in the previous chapter). To understand this, first take the determinants of US exports:

$$X_{us} = f(\$/FX, P_{us}, P_{fx}, Py_{fx}) \qquad\qquad 5.6$$
$$\phantom{X_{us} = f(}+ \quad - \quad + \quad +$$

where X_{us} is US exports, \$/FX is the exchange rate, P_{us} is the US price level, P_{fx} is the foreign price level, and Py_{fx} is foreign nominal income. A rise in either

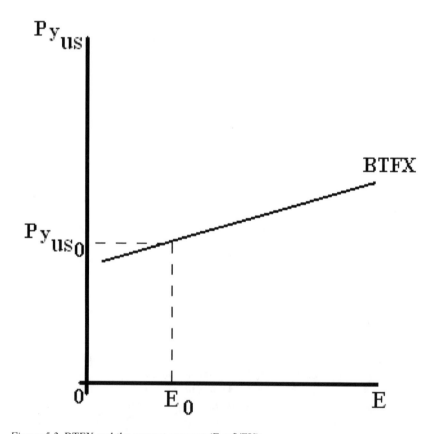

Figure 5.2 BTFX and the current account (E = \$/FX).

$/FX or P_{fx} makes US goods and services more attractive, while a rise in P_{us} makes them less so. A rise in Py_{fx} leads to a rise in foreign consumption, including of US goods and services. Meanwhile, since imports are exports, too, but for the other country, they are determined similarly:

$$M_{us} = f(\$/FX, P_{us}, P_{fx}, Py_{us}) \qquad\qquad 5.7$$
$$\quad\; -\quad\; +\quad -\quad +$$

All variables are defined as above and Py_{us} is US nominal income.

The goal of BTFX is to show those levels of $/FX that would yield $X_{us} = M_{us}$ at various levels of Py_{us}. Any given BTFX holds P_{fx} and Py_{fx} constant, so we are left with $/FX, P_{us}$, and Py_{us} as the relevant variables in the calculation. Since P_{us} is contained within Py_{us} and a rise or fall in either P_{us} or Py_{us} elicits the same directional change in net exports $(X - M)$, we could narrow this list to $/FX and Py_{us} – our axes. Rewriting the above with just these two yields:

$$X_{us} = f(\$/FX) \qquad\qquad 5.8$$
$$\quad\; +$$

$$M_{us} = f(\$/FX, Py_{us}) \qquad\qquad 5.9$$
$$\quad\; -\quad\; +$$

The following conclusions can be drawn from these equations: a rise in $/FX yields an improvement in the US trade balance, while a rise in Py_{us} causes a deterioration. If the question is what $/FX will yield balanced trade at each Py_{us}, then it is clear that as the latter rises (leading to a deterioration in the trade balance), the former must do the same (in order to create an offsetting improvement in the trade balance). Hence the positive slope of BTFX.

Note that, just as in the FX/BOP analysis in the previous chapter, there is no assumption that this will happen in either the short or long run; BTFX is simply a reference, not a locus of equilibrium points. The position of the economy on the axes of this graph will be determined elsewhere in the system and BTFX is used only to decide whether that particular combination creates a trade deficit, surplus, or balance. Points to the right of BTFX are consistent with a trade surplus (and capital account deficit) for the US, while points to the left indicate deficit (and capital surplus).

In terms of the position and slope of BTFX, when it is flatter, this is an indication that trade flows have a relatively greater response to changes in Py than the exchange rate (since a very large change in the latter is required to offset a given change in the former).[5] Were the Py_{fx} to rise, this would necessitate a leftward shift of BTFX (i.e., a stronger home currency at every domestic Py) to offset the rising domestic exports (again, with no assumption that this will happen, just that it would be necessary to generate balanced trade). Last, if the home country's goods and services become more competitive in a way not reflected by E or P_{us}, this will create a leftward shift in BTFX (as net exports would be higher at every Py_{us}, requiring a stronger home country currency for balance).

Returning briefly to the idea that changes in net exports may shift D, this means that as we move to the right or down on the BTFX diagram, so the current account is improving and D shifts up; and as we move to the left or up, D shifts down. Note that shifting D in response to every movement on BTFX can get tedious and not serve to illuminate any new issues. As a consequence, there may be times when this step is skipped.

Figure 5.3 represents the domestic financial sector and is based on an endogenous-money view of the financial system. MM shows all points where the money supply (M^s) is equal to the demand for money (M^d):

$$M^s = M^d$$

5.10

Because we have a fractional-reserve banking system, money is created both exogenously (high-powered money from the central bank, called the monetary base) and endogenously (as banks extend credit). Hence, even without a change in

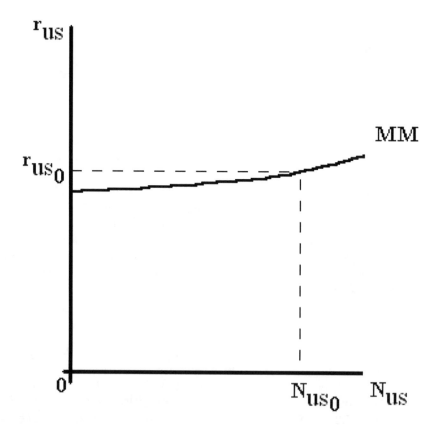

Figure 5.3 Domestic financial sector.

the former, the money supply can fluctuate over a very considerable range via the money multiplier and changes in velocity. When, for example, economic activity is increasing and along with it the demand for money, the supply of the latter may be forthcoming automatically as new loans are extended. When the economy moves into recession and the demand for money is falling, the supply follows as agents repay and default on loans. So, although the monetary base from which banks extend credit is under the control of the central bank, money created by bank loans fluctuates endogenously. These two disparate components of the supply of money are shown in equation 5.11:

$$M^s = M^s_b + M^s_c \qquad\qquad 5.11$$

where M^s_b is that part of the money supply represented by the monetary base and M^s_c is that resulting from the extension of credit by financial institutions.

There is a difference of opinion among Post Keynesians regarding the extent to which money endogeneity operates. Some believe that it is nearly complete, such that the price of liquidity, or the interest rate, remains constant in the face of changes in the demand for money since the latter is always exactly offset by endogenous changes in supply (as caused by M^s_c). At the very least, they argue, because central banks usually target interest rates, even when the endogenous changes (M^s_c) are insufficient the central bank undertakes discretionary policy (M^s_b) to maintain interest-rate stability. This is known as the "horizontalist" view because it posits a horizontal supply curve for money in the standard money-market diagram. Non-horizontalist Post Keynesians accept the endogenous money view, but believe nevertheless that as the demand for liquidity increases, so eventually there is upward pressure on the interest rate. That is the approach taken here, though one could easily adopt the horizontalist view (by simply making MM horizontal or assuming compensating shifts in MM whenever changes in the level of economic activity would otherwise move us from the current rate of interest). Post Keynesian monetary theory argues, incidentally, that in a credit money world such as ours, it is impossible for the supply of money to exceed the demand. Money comes into existence as a portfolio decision: agents consciously borrow from banks or willingly trade assets to the central bank. One cannot compel a situation in which money supply exceeds money demand.

As with M^s, M^d can be broken into two distinct parts:

$$M^d = M^d_l + M^d_h \qquad\qquad 5.12$$

where M^d_l is the demand for money arising from loans and M^d_h is that arising from hoarding. The former occurs when agents want even more cash than currently at their disposal and therefore demand loans; hoarding is the act of holding assets as cash rather that in some other, less liquid, form (bonds, for example). Note that there will be a strong link between M^d_l and M^s_c. When the former rises, this means that agents are approaching banks to request credit. If banks comply, then M^s_c will rise as well. As suggested above, if insufficient reserves exist to accommodate the rise in M^d_1, then it is possible that the central bank may step in and raise M^s_b sufficiently to allow quantity supplied to meet quantity demand at the current interest rate. If not, the latter will rise. Note that the increase in M^s_b need not be as large as the excess quantity demanded because each subsequent rise in M^s_b gives banks excess reserves, allowing them to make new loans and therefore affect M^s_c.

The circumstances surrounding M^d_h are somewhat different. When agents shift toward more liquid assets, this does not create the sort of demand for cash that sets into motion an endogenous increase in supply. Instead, it means that they are choosing not to purchase long-term, illiquid assets that banks could have used as reserves to make new loans. Instead, agents are holding cash. If the central bank does not accommodate the rise in hoarding-associated money demand by raising M^s_b, then this will place upward pressure on the rate of interest as banks both try to induce agents to part with liquidity and charge more for the now-scarce funds that are available for loans. While one would expect M^d_1 to rise when agents were optimistic about the future, M^d_h would rise when they were pessimistic.

Returning to the graph, the price that operates to clear the money market, r_{us}, appears on the vertical axis. As a first approximation, we can say that, ceteris paribus, if the net demand for money rises, MM will rise (meaning a higher interest rate), and if net supply increases, MM falls (meaning a lower one). Unfortunately, the ceteris paribus assumption is a bit difficult to manage here because of the fact that some increases in money demand have the potential to create a concomitant increase in supply. If, for example, $\Delta M^d_1 = \Delta M^s_c$, then a change in the former does not affect the interest rate. But, if banks are unable to accommodate demands and, as a consequence, $\Delta M^d_1 > \Delta M^s_c$, then the very same stimulus leads to a rise in the price of liquidity.

In order to address this problem, the following convention was adopted. First off, assume that the demand for loans increases with the level of economic activity and that the latter is positively correlated with N. This means that as N rises, so will M^d_1 and, therefore, M^s_c. But, in a less-than-horizontal endogenous money world, the latter can only keep up over a limited range. As the N continues to rise, bank reserves are tapped and subsequent rightward movements create increasing pressure in the loans market. The result of this is rising interest rates. This is the reason that MM is drawn rather flat, but with an increasing slope. It reflects the roles of M^d_1 and M^s_c. As suggested above, central bank attempts to target a particular rate of interest can be represented by making MM flatter or, more properly, shifting it sufficiently to maintain the same r_{us}.

Under this arrangement, shifts in MM will be caused by changes in hoarding and the monetary base, while loans and the extension of credit are in the slope of MM. If economic agents shift toward more liquid assets in their portfolio, this would drive MM up and vice versa. Changes in the monetary base might occur as the central bank adjusts interest rate targets or if market conditions necessitate intervention to maintain the current target (as may happen with particular movements in N). An increase in M^s_b shifts MM down. Allowing for international capital, an autonomous rise in unsterilized net inflows would be reflected by a fall in MM; a fall would lead to a rise in MM. Note that, according to some Post Keynesian authors, the likelihood that any such flows would be unsterilized is low (see for example Lavoie 2000, 2001, and 2002–03). In particular, it is thought that net inflows would be used to retire debt (thus keeping the total supply of liquidity constant) while outflows would result in a rise in M^s_c. There is empirical evidence that this does occur at least under some circumstances (Harvey 2004).

The final quadrant (Figure 5.4) is foreign currency market.[6] It is specified:

$$E = f(X_{us}, M_{us}, K^i_{us}, K^o_{us}) \qquad\qquad 5.13$$
$$\quad\ \ - \quad + \quad - \quad +$$

where E is the spot exchange rate (measured as \$/FX), X_{us} is US exports, M_{us} is US imports, K^i_{us} is US capital inflows (sales of US assets to foreigners), and K^o_{us} is US capital outflows (US purchases of foreign assets). Each act that requires trading foreign currency for dollars (X_{us} and K^i_{us}) represents a demand for that currency and leads to a dollar appreciation (a fall in E), while each act that requires trading dollars for foreign currency (M_{us} and K^o_{us}) represents supply and thus causes a dollar depreciation (a rise in E, or \$/FX).

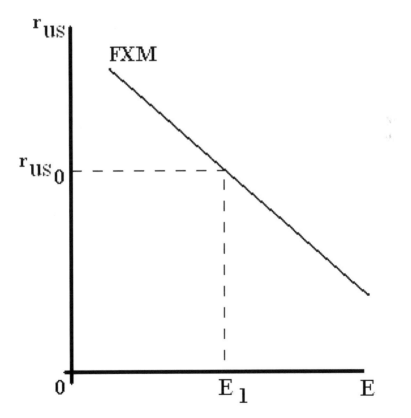

Figure 5.4 Foreign currency market (E = \$/FX).

As suggested in earlier chapters, trade flows, except insofar as they affect agents' portfolio decisions, tend to be relatively minor determinants of currency prices. Hence, since a two-dimensional graphical analysis limits to one the number of independent variables we can explicitly portray in the model (given that the other axis is used to show the dependent variable), a determinant related to capital flows will be selected. Furthermore, the forces driving the latter will be assumed to be interest rates and agents' expectations of future currency movements, or $(\$/FX)^e$:

$$(K^i_{us} - K^o_{us}) = f(r_{us}, r_{fx}, (\$/FX)^e) \qquad\qquad 5.14$$
$$\phantom{(K^i_{us} - K^o_{us}) = f(} + \quad - \quad\; -$$

The assumption here is that as US interest rates rise, so US assets become more attractive; as foreign interest rates rise, so US assets become less attractive, and as the expected value of the dollar declines (a fall in $(\$/FX)^e$), market participants shift away from US assets and toward foreign ones.

Because r_{us} would be on the vertical axis of a graph in the upper-left quadrant, it can be used as the explicit determinant of net capital flows and, hence, exchange rates. This is especially useful because relative interest rates play a very important role in currency price movements. The function for the exchange rate portion of the model is labeled FXM and is shown in Figure 5.4. Its negative slope is a result of the fact that a rise in US interest rates leads to a dollar appreciation (fall in E or $\$/FX$) as agents buy the dollar in order to obtain US interest-bearing assets. A rise in r_{fx} does the opposite as agents substitute foreign bonds for US ones, shifting FXM to the right. Last, when agents upwardly revise $(\$/FX)^e$, this leads to a shift away from US assets and a fall in the dollar (i.e. a rightward shift in FXM and a rise in E or $\$/FX$). Much more will be said about the determinants of market participants' expectations later in this chapter.

Focusing solely on the three variables from equation 5.14 means that the current account is being ignored. And, indeed, it often will be in the analysis that follows. It is a relatively small factor in the market (except possibly as a variable driving $(\$/FX)^e$) and shifting FXM every time there is a change in trade flows will be tedious and have only a marginal effect on the events elsewhere in the diagram. However, if it is deemed necessary, FXM can move left whenever net domestic exports rise and move right when they fall.

Whether or not the exchange rate that prevails is to be associated with a capital account surplus or deficit depends on the position of the balanced trade exchange rate as shown in BTFX. If the rate that prevails on FXM is to the right of the rate shown on BTFX (given Py_{us}), then a trade surplus and capital account deficit result; if it is to the left, then a trade deficit and capital account surplus follow.

Figure 5.5 shows the complete open-economy Z-D diagram. Beginning with employment and output on the bottom right, the D curve cuts Z at (Py_{us0}, N_{us0}). According to BTFX, this means that the exchange rate must be equal to E_0 if trade is to be balanced. However, that is not the case in Figure 5.5. The current level of employment combined with money-market conditions as represented on MM yields an interest rate of r_{us0}, which means that in actuality the exchange rate is

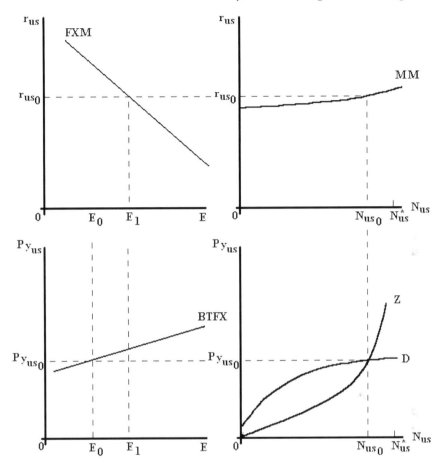

Figure 5.5 Post Keynesian open-economy Z-D diagram (E = $/FX).

E_1. At that price, the dollar is cheap and hence the US experiences a trade surplus and a capital account deficit. Note further that the economy is at less-than-full employment (the full-employment level being marked by N^*_{us}).

One last point to be made is that it is assumed that reactions to stimuli in the FXM and MM quadrants are likely to take place faster than those in the Z-D quadrant. For example, a change in the interest rate target by the central monetary authority can be expected to result in an immediate shift in MM, which would be quickly followed by a movement along FXM as the exchange rate adjusted to the new interest rate, but any resulting change in the balance of trade caused by the exchange rate movement, though immediately plotted in the BTFX space, would impact on D only after the passage of some time.

Now consider a number of scenarios with this new framework. First, take for example a rise in investment (due perhaps to an increase in π^e). This would lead to an upward shift in D, raising both N_{us} and Py_{us} (as shown on Figure 5.6 – note

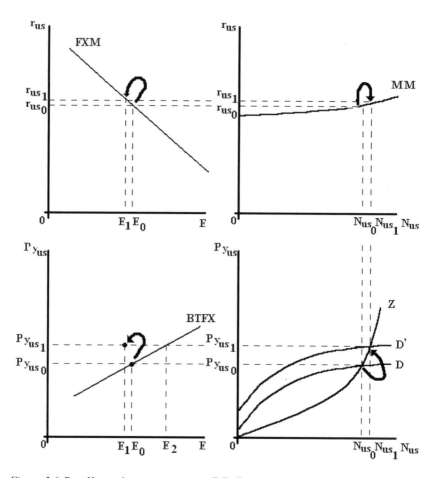

Figure 5.6 Post Keynesian open-economy Z-D diagram, rise in investment (E = \$/FX).

that the initial conditions assume balanced trade since at E_0). According to BTFX, the rise in Py_{us} to Py_{us1} means that the dollar would have to be weaker – E_2 rather than E_0 – if trade were to remain balanced. But, the actual exchange rate moves in the opposite direction (from E_0 to E_1) because interest rates rise slightly (due to the increase in the level of economic activity).[7] Hence, the dollar appreciation combined with the increase in the level of economic activity, and therefore imports, causes the trade account to move into deficit. A fiscal stimulus would have an analogous impact to rising investment. *The bottom line is that, in this model, economic expansion is correlated with a fall in net exports and a domestic currency appreciation – precisely what we observe in the real world.* Note also that the rise in D would be muted by the fall in net exports and that, since the latter implies a rise in net capital inflows, the rise in r_{us} would be tempered (as will the dollar appreciation). Net, however, we should observe the movements illustrated.

Last, given that the rise in Py_{us} was not exclusively inflationary (something we can assume since N_{us} rose), it might also be the case that FXM would shift to the left as agents revise their exchange-rate expectations to predict a stronger dollar, adding to the pressures created by the initial change. But, none of these addenda would alter the overall picture as illustrated.

A rightward shift in Z would have a similar impact on the above since it would raise both N and Py. However, it may be accompanied by a leftward shift in BTFX if the shift in Z resulted from a fall in wages or a rise in productivity. This is so because it can be expected to increase the nation's competitiveness in the market for goods and services and so a stronger dollar would be needed to maintain balanced trade. It would also be reasonable, depending on the extent of the increase in competitiveness, to then shift BTFX sufficiently to yield a US trade surplus (despite the dollar appreciation and the rise in Py_{us}).

A change in monetary policy is illustrated in Figure 5.7. This creates conflicting

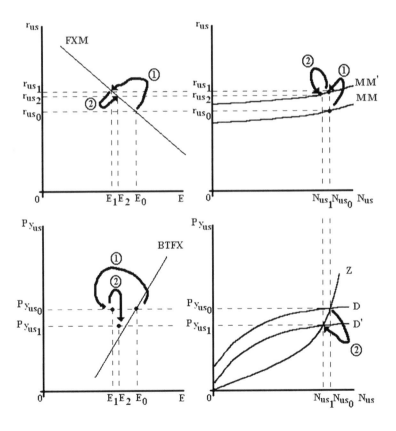

Figure 5.7 Post Keynesian open-economy Z-D diagram, rise in interest rates (E = \$/FX).

pressures, one set of forces manifesting itself relatively quickly and the other not until later. Say that the central monetary authority acts to raise domestic interest rates. The first effect is on the MM curve in the upper right quadrant (shown in Figure 5.7 as ①), which is shifted upwards. According to the FXM curve, this will lead to a net inflow of financial capital and a domestic currency appreciation from E_0 to E_1 (the effect of this net inflow is assumed to be either already reflected in the shift of MM or sterilized).[8] The BTFX diagram shows that this will lead to a trade deficit (assuming E_0 to be the balanced-trade exchange rate at Py_{us0}).

The rising interest rate and trade deficit will then begin to affect the D curve, the former via investment and the latter through net exports.[9] In both instances, the impact will be a fall in D, leading to a decline in employment and a reversal of the rise in the interest rate (all the movements marked by a ② in Figure 5.7 represent the shift in D and the consequences thereof). This also means that the domestic currency appreciation may be dampened (as shown by the move from E_1 to E_2). However, there are reasons to believe that this impact is smaller in absolute value (perhaps substantially so) than the initial currency appreciation since trade flows are known to be price inelastic and interest rates a secondary factor (to the expectation of profit from investment, or π^e) in determining physical investment. In addition, if the rising interest rates created the net capital inflows which then caused the dollar appreciation, the trade balance (in the absence of official intervention) must logically have worsened.[10] We end, therefore, at N_{us1}, r_{us1}, and E_2 and with the US experiencing a trade deficit.

The examples thus far have shown the impact of an event in the Z-D or MM quadrants. Perhaps more interesting, particularly because Neoclassical models downplay this possibility (except as a short-run phenomenon), is an exogenous shift in market expectations. Say, for example, that the chair of the US Federal Reserve makes a speech in which it is implied that US interest rates will be lowered over the course of the next six months. At that moment, absolutely nothing has changed on Z-D, MM, or BTFX. It is likely, however, that agents now expect the dollar to depreciate and FXM will therefore shift to the right to reflect this belief. As agents divest themselves of dollar assets, so the spot dollar falls (\$/FX moves from E_0 to E_1). This is shown as ① in the FXM quadrant on Figure 5.8. Moving to the BTFX quadrant, it is evident that the new exchange rate yields a US trade surplus (and a capital account deficit) since E_1 is greater than the balanced-trade exchange rate, E_0.

Eventually, this in turn will lead to an upward shift in D (to D'), which raises N_{us} and Py_{us} (though with the typical elasticities involved the magnitudes may be small). If MM is not horizontal over this range, r will also rise, causing a slight dollar appreciation (from E_1 to E_2). For the same reason as cited in the previous example (i.e., the trade surplus will not be terribly large given its price inelasticity) it is assumed that the reversal of the dollar's initial movement is smaller in absolute value so that, even with the movement of the actual and balanced-trade exchange rates towards one another, there is still a trade surplus.[11] These secondary movements are marked as ②. The final resting place is N_{us1}, r_{us1}, and E_2, with the US experiencing a trade surplus. *All this occurs in response to a change in what was*

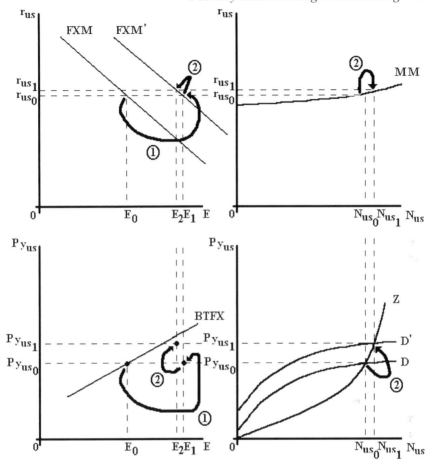

Figure 5.8 Post Keynesian open-economy Z-D diagram, fall in the expected value of the dollar (E = $/FX).

expected. Regardless of whether or not that expectation turns out to be warranted, real economic outcomes are created by those expectations. And if the forecast turns out to be wrong, the economy does not magically shunt itself back onto the growth path that would have been followed had there been perfect foresight. The long run is simply the aggregation of short runs and the expectation that the dollar would fall has shifted the economy onto a new path.

These few examples show the role of the currency price in a Post Keynesian open-economy framework. There are no mechanisms pushing trade toward balance or output toward the full-employment level, the portfolio capital market is the driving force behind currency movements, and expectations are permitted a causal role and can, by themselves, affect output and employment. If we accept Thirlwall's (among others') contention that trade balances are more sensitive to income than price/exchange rate effects, then BTFX should be drawn very flat (as in Figures 5.6 and 5.8, but unlike Figure 5.7) and for those suffering from a balance-of-payments-growth constraint, the actual exchange rate should lie quite a distance to the left of the BTFX. In addition, the sort of movements capable of yielding significant changes in net exports would be more likely to arise from the factors that shift BTFX rather than changes in E or Py. Chapter Six will show several more examples of the Z-D, open economy diagram as it is used to explain fluctuations in the post-Bretton Woods dollar.

FOREIGN EXCHANGE MARKET PSYCHOLOGY: THE MENTAL MODEL

The above leaves exchange rate expectations as exogenous. But, because portfolio capital flows are the primary drivers of currency prices and because agents' forecasts are the major determinants of those capital flows, a well-developed model of expectations formation is vital to understanding foreign exchange rate determination. The dynamic nature of this process requires the use of a schematic rather than a general equilibrium model. Arrows will indicate a line of causation from the base to the head. A plus sign under the arrow means a positive correlation such that the direction of change of the variable at the base is transmitted to that at the head (i.e., a rise (fall) in the base becomes a rise (fall) in the head). A negative sign means a negative correlation so that the direction of change reverses (a rise becomes a fall, and fall is transmitted as a rise). A question mark implies that further information is required to determine the impact of the base on the head.

Agents generate two sets of expectations: short-term and medium-term, where the latter (which may also be called an "attractor") become a sort of lens through which agents filter inputs (Schulmeister 1987, 1988). Though actors may have a specific level of the exchange rate in mind when forming medium-term expectations, it is best thought of as taking one of three values with respect to a particular currency: bullish (pro the currency in question), bearish (anti the currency in question), or neutral. When medium-term expectations are bullish, the significance of events that would lead to appreciation is magnified and the significance of those that would end in depreciation is discounted. Bearishness has an analogous impact, while neutrality means that no particular attractor exists. For example, if it is announced that a nation's interest rates are likely to rise (which is typically seen as an indicator of future appreciation) and the attractor with respect to that exchange rate is currently bullish, a large increase in the value of the currency is likely; however, had the attractor been bearish, then the same announcement would have less impact and might even be entirely ignored. In addition, when the import of events appears to match the attractor, agents' confidence is increased.

As one might suspect, the attractor is a function of a moving average of the factors driving the short-run expectations.[12] In other words, as data accumulate on one side of the issue (i.e., appreciation or depreciation), so the medium-term expectation gradually shifts. This is particularly true when bandwagon effects are strong. Thus, the determinants of the short-term forecast and the attractor can be discussed together even though the specific manner in which they affect the dependent variable differs somewhat (with the short-term forecast reacting rather quickly to inputs and the attractor doing so only after a trend emerges). In the figures that follow, the medium-term expectation is shown as an exogenous variable placed off to one side, but in fact it is affected by a moving average of the short-term forecast. I chose not to show such a link for simplicity.

Before continuing, three facts regarding the short-term forecast, the attractor, and the factors driving them should be recalled: 1) expectations are not independent of the objective variable – they determine it; 2) expectations of the future impact the spot price immediately (the magnitude of the effect being a function of the difference between the expected and spot rates and the level of agents' confidence in the forecast); and 3) if expectations are the ultimate driver of currency prices, the market could be moved by *whatever* agents decide is important, from changes in real GDP to sun spots.

As it turns out, currency market participants are not nearly as capricious as the last point suggests they could be. That they are not is a function of the fact that they are guided by the worldview of the subculture of which they are members. That worldview recognizes what was established in Chapter Three – that there exist (outside of official intervention) only three reasons to purchase foreign currency: importation of foreign goods and services, direct foreign investment, and portfolio foreign investment. Agents' perception of those processes is what forms their mental model and, therefore, their expectations.[13] Figure 5.9 shows this portion of the market participants' mental model, where $(X - M)^e_{us}$ is expected net exports, net DFI^e_{us} is expected net direct foreign investment into the US, net PFI^e_{us} is expected

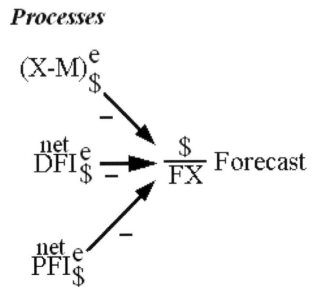

Figure 5.9 Mental model: processes.

net portfolio foreign investment into the US, and $/FX Forecast is the exchange rate expectation. Note that each of the determinants is assumed to create a net demand for the dollar and hence a dollar appreciation (fall in $/FX). This is the reason for the negative link between each of the three processes and the forecast. If $(X - M)^e_{us}$, net DFI^e_{us}, or net PFI^e_{us} rise, then $/FX Forecast falls, and vice versa. Note, too, that each process is, by virtue of the "e" superscript, what agents expect to occur. Realized levels of $(X - M)$, DFI, and PFI are obviously important foci for their expectational counterparts, but for a number of reasons are unreliable as the sole inputs into a forecast (not least important being the fact that in many cases the realized values will not be known for at least one month after the event when estimates are released).

Figure 5.10 adds those base factors upon which processes depend. Those factors are $(r_{us} - r_{fx})^e$, or expected relative interest rates (US minus foreign); $(y_{us} - y_{fx})^e$, expected macroeconomic growth and stability (US minus foreign); $(P_{us} - P_{fx})^e$, expected prices (US minus foreign); and, expected $ liquidity.[14] The links are to be understood as follows. The expectation of rising (relative) prices impacts negatively on agents' forecast of net US exports as imports would become cheaper and exports more expensive; prices are also a negative force with respect to net DFI^e_{us} as vertical (resource seeking) direct foreign investment is discouraged by increasing input costs. Changes in the prices of goods and services have no direct impact on portfolio investment and so no link between them is shown. Expectations of rising (relative) macro growth and stability would cause agents to forecast a fall in net exports (as rising incomes lead to greater volumes of imports for the US), a rise in net DFI^e_{us} (as horizontal direct foreign investment goes in search of markets), and a rise in net PFI^e_{us}. The last results for three reasons. First, asset issuers will

Base Factors

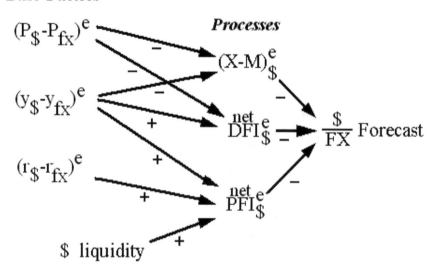

Figure 5.10 Mental model: processes, and base factors.

be more likely to earn profits in an environment of macro growth and stability, raising the value of securities they have sold. Second, at least part of the rising domestic incomes may be diverted into the asset market, driving up prices. Third, government-issued securities increase in value because as the tax base grows this diminishes the likelihood of default. Rising (relative) interest rates have no direct connection to net exports or direct foreign investment, but, ceteris paribus, make assets more attractive to investors and lead to portfolio capital inflows (net PFI^e_{us}). Finally, the expected ease with which an asset can be converted into a form that retires debt or purchases goods, services, and other assets (i.e., its liquidity) relative to other assets is an important consideration for portfolio investors. In addition to asset-specific factors, liquidity increases if the currency in which the asset is denominated is one in which many commodities are priced or if it is the de facto or de jure international reserve currency (the dollar has benefited from both of these since World War Two, though it may be rapidly losing ground).The ultimate impact of every base factor on the currency price forecast is unambiguous with the exception of macro growth and stability. While a rise in expected $(y_{us} - y_{fx})^e$ would lead agents to expect a fall in net exports, thus depressing the domestic currency price, it simultaneously leads to a rise in both net DFI^e_{us} and net PFI^e_{us}. In practice, however, because agents believe that capital flows dominate international transactions, rising expected macro growth and stability tends to drive forecast domestic currency values higher (though one can identify occasions when rising GDP is thought to be a negative through net exports – see, for example, Bretton Woods Collapse and Adjustment in the next chapter).

Figure 5.11 adds the final piece to the mental model: indicators. This set represents the evolving set of variables thought to reflect, affect, or predict the base factors and sometimes the processes themselves. Some members of this set have

Mental Model

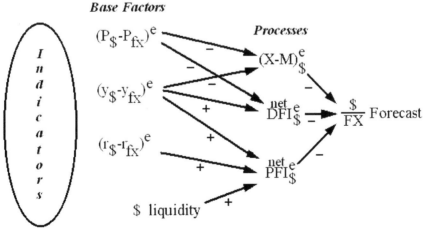

Figure 5.11 Complete mental model: processes, base factors, and indicators.

played constant and predictable roles for many years (unemployment, for example), while others come and go (such as monetary aggregates). Agents will monitor these indicators, along with the base factors and processes, and use them to form their forecasts. A position is then taken in the market and today's exchange rate is thereby determined. Note that for many, if not all, agents, one of the indicators will be the signals given by technical trading rules. Because of their unique role, however, I opted to show them separately from indicators (technical analysis will be added to the model in Figure 5.12).

Agents use the complete mental model shown in 5.11 to develop their forecasts. In general, they start at the left and move right. Market participants pick up clues from the various indicators and use them to predict the movements of the base factors. This then feeds into the forecast of the processes, and finally the exchange rate itself.

It is not necessary for every input into the expectation formation process to enter at the far left; in fact, agents would rather that they did not since less remains to be interpreted if the diagram can be short cut. For example, the US the trade balance is reported monthly. Last month's reported $(X - M)$ can feed directly into the forecast of next month's $(X - M)^e_{us}$. In addition to preferring to enter the mental model as close to $/FX Forecast as possible, agents would also rather use variables that are reported frequently and are straightforward to interpret. And those impacting on portfolio investment will receive extra weight because of the dominant role that process plays in the market. Historically, these preferences with respect to the mental model components have meant that interest rates have played the central role in expectation formation. They allow some shortcut of the mental model and are reported continuously, easy to interpret, and affect portfolio investment. The second most important focus has been unemployment. Though it is an indicator and thus enters the mental model at the far left, it is easy to interpret, reported monthly, and affects portfolio investment through macro growth and stability (GDP growth rates are also monitored but are not reported as frequently). Net exports come in third. Though obviously not PFI, they are reported monthly and enter the mental model at the process stage, hence very close to the dependent variable. Last, inflation has often been a focus as well, though not consistently so. Again, though it is not concerned with portfolio capital flows, consumer and producer price data are reported monthly and are an unambiguous negative in the mental model. Actually, it is not uncommon for inflation to be interpreted as an indicator of future interest rate movements (with rising inflation thought to trigger central bank tightening). This would cause it to play a dual role, both as shown explicitly in Figure 5.11 and as a member of the set of indicators (one positively correlated with future interest rates). *These four (interest rates, unemployment, trade balance, and inflation) have formed the core indicators, base factors, and processes considered by agents in forming their forecasts in the post-Bretton Woods era.* If we are considering short time horizons, then technical analysis is properly considered as well (trading rules are created in real time and are easily interpreted).

Before leaving this topic it would be useful to spend a little time considering how the set of variables labeled "indicators" in Figure 5.11 evolve over time.

Many may come and go as members of that set. The structure of the mental model is based on experience and professional and scholarly research. That experience and research exists within a particular social context so that events and processes are filtered by the world view shared by the market participants. In aggregate, they are free to choose whatever they want as their foci, but such freedom does not exist at the individual level, particularly since those whose forecasts deviate from the average will be punished. Thus, what comprises "indicators" is socially sanctioned.

That which is sanctioned may evolve over time and there are four factors associated with that evolution: regime change, structural change, academic and professional theory, and forecast error. Regime change can lead agents to revise their forecasting model. This occurs when they believe that policy makers have altered their standard responses to given economic circumstances. In that case, agents may adjust their forecasts to take this into account. For example, after aggressive anti-inflationary stances were adopted by many governments in the late 1970s/early 1980s, many agents began to associate spikes in prices with corresponding increases in future real interest rates. Hence, rather than leading to currency depreciation due to the decline in the purchasing power of the money, inflation often caused appreciations.

Structural change has a similar effect. As the links among the variables in the macroeconomy are thought to have evolved, agents may take this into account. New and different factors may become a focus, while older, obsolete ones drop out. As capital flows have come to dominate trade flows, for instance, so one would expect agents' attention to shift from indicators of the latter to those of the former.

In addition, innovations in academic and professional theories regarding the operation of foreign exchange rates may lead to changes in mental models. Note that these need not have any connection with regime or structural changes. New fads and trends among scholars and practitioners are not uncommon and are sufficient by themselves to cause a re-evaluation of the variables used in agents' forecasts. For example, the rising popularity of monetarism over the 1960s and 1970s led to an increased reliance on monetary aggregates in predictions. No one, least of all the monetarists themselves, believed that readers were being alerted to a change in policy or the structure of the economy; it was simply that, in their minds, the true nature of the economy had not theretofore been properly described.

Forecast error provides a motivation rather than a guideline for re-evaluation of "indicators." There will be agents who were out of step, some more often than others and everyone at some point. This means that while the average expectation is always right in the sense that it causes an immediate currency price adjustment in the forecast direction, a large group of agents is nevertheless constantly working to improve their forecast because they did not predict the correct direction or magnitude.

In summary, the community of those participating in the foreign exchange market is a distinct subculture with mores, sanctions, worldviews, status, et cetera. Because they dominate the market, whatever they think is true becomes fact as it then moves the market. Their subculture views itself as highly technical and logical and its members are serious students of economics. There is, therefore, a stronger link between what are sometimes called "fundamental" factors in the market for foreign currency and currency prices than is necessary given the domination of exchange rates by capital flows and agents' expectations. This is a function of the fact that agents think fundamentals (however defined) are important and hence focus on them to at least some extent. But, the fundamentals really are not determining the prices; it is market participants' evolving and uncertain interpretation of them that is doing so.

Returning to Figure 5.11, though it completes the mental model, five factors are omitted: technical analysis, bandwagon, cash in, medium-term expectations, and forecast confidence. These are added in Figure 5.12, the augmented mental model. Note that this new diagram assumes that the direct effect of changes in the forecast value of the dollar is on actual PFI into the U.S (net PFI_{us}). As agents expect the dollar to gain value (which corresponds to a fall in $/FX Forecast), so they purchase US financial assets (rise in net PFI_{us}). This then leads to an actual dollar appreciation (a fall in $/FX).

The basic effect of technical analysis (which is shown as "technical analysis buy $ signal") is that it will tend to cause forecasts to assume continued exchange rate movements in the same direction. As $/FX falls, for example, so trading rules (most of which are based on some variation of a moving average) trigger signals that indicate further falls. Agents will take this into account in their forecasts, especially over shorter time horizons, and it is thus fed into FX Forecast. The effect of bandwagon (expressed as "bandwagon purchases of US assets") is similar to that of technical analysis, except that it does not enter directly into the forecast but affects portfolio capital flows. As agents observe assets appreciating (via a fall in $/FX, for example, which signals a dollar appreciation and thus a rise in the value of US assets), for reasons explained in Chapter Three, they buy those assets (hence

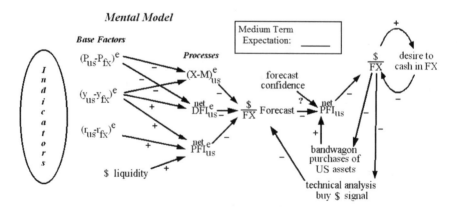

Figure 5.12 Augmented mental model including medium-term expectation, technical analysis, bandwagon, confidence, and cash in.

the negative link from $/FX to "bandwagon purchases of US financial assets"). Cash in, also explained in Chapter Three, occurs when agents become anxious to realize heretofore paper profits. This is shown as a negative feedback loop, with an appreciating foreign currency (rising $/FX) increasing the "desire to cash in FX." This then, assuming cash in occurs, leads to a reversal of the direction on $/FX (i.e., FX depreciates). It is important to note that this process has no net effect over longer time horizons – it creates white noise around a trend. By contrast, a trend is exactly what medium-term expectations (noted in the box on Figure 5.12) create. As suggested at the beginning of this section, it acts as a lens through which information is filtered. When market sentiment is strongly pro-dollar, dollar data that suggest depreciation may be downplayed or even ignored. In the meantime, the impact of positive dollar signals is magnified. One cannot properly understand the operation of the mental model without taking this into account. Note, finally, that over time, movements in $/FX Forecast may change the medium-term forecast and that the latter is especially likely to move in the face of strong bandwagon effects. As this connection makes itself felt over a longer time horizon than assumed elsewhere on the diagram I elected not to show this explicitly.

The last new factor to be added is forecast confidence, which enters as a variable with an indeterminate effect on net PFI_{us} (marked by "?" on the schematic). Actually, it is very clear how it impacts but it is difficult to show in this format. It has been argued heretofore that once agents form a forecast, they buy or sell foreign and domestic assets depending on which currency they expect to see appreciate. That act then causes the spot currency price to move in the direction of the forecast. However, there are reasons to believe that even after this takes place, there may still be a gap between what agents in aggregate expect and where the spot price has come to rest. The key here is confidence. If, for example, market participants expect a dollar appreciation but have misgivings, then the corresponding rise in net PFI_{us} may be very small, leading to little change in the current $/FX. Thus, in equilibrium, there will be a gap between $/FX Forecast and $/FX, a gap that is an inverse function of the level of confidence. Were agents to have complete confidence in their forecast, then the change in net PFI_{us} will be exactly enough to drive $/FX to the same level as $/FX Forecast.

In sum, the three feedback loops – cash in, bandwagon effects, and technical analysis – are key to behavior. It is because of them that, in general, currency markets tend to move under their own momentum (due to bandwagon and technical analysis), interrupted by brief reversals caused by cash in. Cash in causes a zigzag pattern; if bandwagon and technical analysis have imparted a particular direction to the market, the zigzag occurs around that vector. As market participants work with their mental model to interpret the impact of events (base factors and indicators) on the processes (thus generating their short-term and medium-term forecasts), so the zigzagging vector may be turned in new directions. The next round of actual (X – M), DFI, and PFI must then adjust to the newly determined $/FX and to any volatility that is created. Again, expectations create reality. Chapter Six will work through a number of examples of the application of the mental model and ZD diagram to real-world events.

UNCOVERED INTEREST RATE PARITY

That the confidence gap can be fairly large is the key to solving a long-standing puzzle in Neoclassical economics: the failure of uncovered interest rate parity (discussed in Chapter Two) to hold in the real world. Why should it not be true that expected rates of return on like interest-bearing assets throughout the world are equal once forecast exchange-rate movements are taken into account? Recall equation (2.4'):

$$(1+r_s) = (FX/\$)(1+r_{FX})(\$/FX)^e \qquad\qquad 2.4'$$

The most common Neoclassical suggestion as to why empirical evidence is not supportive of this relationship in the real world is that there exists a risk premium attached to one country or the other. In that event, even in equilibrium the assets of the riskier nation must be expected to earn a higher return. If not, capital will flow from that risky nation to the other, driving the former's interest rates higher and the latter's lower (and bidding up the value of the latter's currency).

This very reasonable argument runs into trouble, however, because not only does experience indicate that the risk premium changes with more frequency than one would have expected, but no one has been able to find a reasonable explanation for the particular manner in which risk (if that is truly what we are observing) varies in the real world. In other words, it is not clear why macroeconomic fundamentals would lead, for example, the US to be viewed by the market as more risky than Germany one year, and the opposite the next. The observed patterns do not make sense if they are being driven solely by risk. A further puzzle is the fact that what one often sees is that the deviation from uncovered interest rate parity follows interest rate changes. When US interest rates rise relative to German, so the uncovered interest rate deviation moves toward favoring US interest-bearing assets (i.e., a higher expected rate of return on US interest-bearing assets), and vice versa. In fact, it is not at all uncommon for higher interest rates in one country than another to correspond to the expectation that the former's currency will appreciate relative to the latter's – precisely the opposite of uncovered interest rate parity's prediction.

The problem with the Neoclassical version of interest rate parity is that it assumes complete confidence in the forecast $(\$/FX)^e$. If agents are, because they are unsure, less anxious to "put their money where their mouth is," then it is very likely that the capital flows that serve as the adjustment mechanism will not occur in sufficient volume to set the two sides of the equation equal. In fact, given the level of uncertainty in the market, such a complete adjustment would be the exception rather than the rule.

Note that if the culprit is lack of confidence rather than risk (not to deny that the latter could not play some role), then it is impossible to say a priori which country's expected return may exceed the other's. With risk, the riskier country's assets must promise the higher return; but lack of confidence simply says that there will be a gap that agents lack the courage to close – it can favor either country.

This is analogous to the pattern of gold prices when there are transportation costs. If gold sells for \$35/oz in location A and it costs \$5/oz to transport it to location B, then gold can sell for as much as \$40/oz or as low as \$30/oz in B. But, if it goes beyond those bounds, it becomes profitable to undertake arbitrage, which enforces the range set by the transportation cost. In the case of uncovered interest-rate parity, it is not transportation costs that discourage the flows but lack of complete confidence in the forecast.

Now consider this: keeping the gold-price analogy, if the price in both A and B happens to be \$35/oz and the transportation costs \$5/oz, then whatever might happen in the gold markets in either nation can create a deviation up to the point that it is large enough to compensate for the transportation cost. If new gold discoveries in B drive the price down to \$33/oz, the market between A and B is still in equilibrium. Likewise, as a nation's interest rates rise or fall so the deviation from uncovered interest rate parity will follow, just as long as the movement that is created is not sufficiently large to offset agents' lack of confidence and thereby trigger capital flows. *This is precisely the pattern we observe in the real world.* Uncovered interest rate parity deviations tend to follow interest rate movements. This simply cannot be explained using risk alone.

This view, incidentally, is not inconsistent with the Post Keynesian theory that domestic interest rates across countries are largely independent of one another due to public or private market sterilization of capital flows (referenced earlier in this chapter).[15] In the event that the former occurs, the idea is that governments, seeking to maintain target interest rates, may engage in exogenous adjustment of the money supply designed to exactly offset net capital flows. In the case of the latter, if the expected rate of return in one country exceeds that in another then in an endogenous money economy it is quite reasonable to expect the inflows in the high-return country to be automatically sterilized as agents use the new funds to retire debt (meanwhile, in the low-return country the outgoing flow is offset by the creation of new money as the private sector issues new debt). The sterilization means that interest rates remain constant despite the flow of capital that is occurring. But without the addition of the concept of less-than-complete forecast confidence, this explanation of the empirical failure of interest rate parity is valid only in fixed exchange rate regimes. Otherwise, the private-market led sterilization only prevents the interest rates from adjusting; spot exchange rates would be free to do so and thus maintain interest rate parity.

CURRENCY AND FINANCIAL CRISES

The most dramatic event in a currency market is catastrophic depreciation. The Asian (1997) and Mexican (1994) crises manifested themselves as precipitous falls in the values of the currencies of the nations involved. In the case of the former, "the number of Asians living in absolute poverty more than doubled in countries without elaborate social safety nets, and pockets of absolute poverty reappeared in Korea and Thailand" (Jackson 1999: 2). Mexico experienced a severe recession, a spike in unemployment, and a shift onto a less-advantageous growth path. Such events are clearly more than white noise and if the modern international monetary economy is to be understood properly then these episodes must be explained. Doing so requires moving beyond, though not ignoring, the open-economy, Z-D and mental-model diagrams. In particular, it will be necessary to take a closer look at how financial markets evolve both over the business cycle and once bandwagons emerge.

One of the reasons that crises have been a challenge to explain is that they are not all alike. In the model that follows, it is hypothesized that they may emerge in one of three distinct tension points in the economy: the currency-price divergence point, the financial-returns divergence point, and the financial-fragility point. Once any one of these reaches a critical level, a catastrophic deflation can result which may then spread throughout the macroeconomy and trigger one or both of the other tension points. These will be addressed in turn.

Currency-price divergence occurs because bandwagon effects pull the spot exchange rate away from the level consistent with the mental model's forecast. Note that Figure 5.12 shows that bandwagon effects can move a currency price via net capital flows. Most of the time, the feedback loop traced by net PFI_{us}, $/FX, and bandwagon purchases of US assets will simply be one of the many factors driving currency prices. There are occasions, however, when it takes over and becomes the core driver, with signals generated by trading rules and a sympathetic medium-term expectation adding fuel to the fire and causing contrary indicators emerging from the mental model to be downplayed or ignored. This can occur over hours, days, or months. Such bandwagon-dominated runs are, consistent with the availability heuristic, most common when the initial price increase is sudden, steep, and initiated by a dramatic event (Kindleberger 2000). Post Keynesians see financial liberalization programs as a common candidate for the latter, particularly in the developing world (see for example Cruz, Amann, and Walters 2006). The point of separation between the actual exchange rate and the mental model's shadow forecast – the currency-price divergence point – may eventually become so large that many market participants even see and understand that these two forces are in conflict, but lack the confidence to swim against the stream. Furthermore, so long as the boom continues, there is money to be made by following the crowd. The game becomes one of guessing how long the boom can be sustained, and when to jump.

The larger that gap becomes, the more precarious the situation and the more unremarkable may be the incident necessary to start the slide. Depending on the degree of divergence that had evolved, the reversal can be quite dramatic as agents rush to divest themselves of what they have now decided is a seriously overvalued money. The collapse itself could thereby be the sudden, dramatic event that starts a bandwagon run in the other direction.

Figure 5.13 illustrates this process (note that it shares some variables with the mental model). Starting with "total net demand for domestic assets," this is the combined (foreign and domestic) demand for private and public financial assets of the economy in question (minus corresponding supply). As this rises, so it should

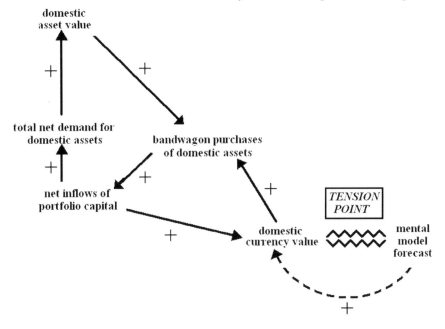

Figure 5.13 Currency crises: currency-forecast divergence under a flexible exchange rate regime.

drive up the value of those assets (shown as "domestic asset values"); and, as it falls, so those values should fall. In addition, rising domestic asset values may lead to bandwagon purchases. Though such purchases will be undertaken by both domestic and foreign agents, since the goal of this model is to show the impact of an asset boom on the currency market only the latter is shown. They are reflected in "net inflows of portfolio capital" and when this increases, so does "total net demand for domestic assets."

This completes the left-hand feedback loop on Figure 5.13, which shows the manner in which a domestic asset boom (or bust) may be driven by a bandwagon. The second feedback loop in the diagram shows the effect on the currency market. Because those foreigners purchasing the domestic assets must first obtain the domestic currency, net inflows of portfolio capital lead necessarily to a rise in "domestic currency value." And since the latter directly and positively affects the value of those assets to foreigners, the appreciating currency fuels the bandwagon purchases.

Together, these two feedback loops may operate to push domestic asset and currency values higher and higher. The complications created by the former will be addressed momentarily; with respect to the latter, this contributes to the currency-forecast divergence point as the spot exchange rate moves increasingly out of line with the mental-model forecast. The dashed line between that forecast and domestic currency value on Figure 5.13 is intended to show that there is normally a link there (as there is in Figure 5.12), but that when a crisis is building that link is broken. The larger the distance, the greater the tension, and the more unremarkable may be the incident necessary to start the collapse.

Note that in the case of a fixed exchange rate, the same fundamental forces are at work but the manner in which they manifest themselves is different. This is illustrated on Figure 5.14. Added are three new cells: pegged domestic currency value, sustainability of the peg, and foreign reserves. In addition, one cell has been altered – domestic currency value is now "free-market domestic currency value," or the value that would have prevailed under a float. Also, the tension point has been moved. One of the central premises here is that the further a pegged rate is from its erstwhile floating value, the less likely are officials perceived as being able to defend that rate (given a particular volume of foreign reserves, as shown). If speculators come to view an exchange rate as hopelessly overvalued, they will attack it and force devaluation or a float. Hence, as GAP on Figure 5.14 rises (holding "foreign reserves" constant), "sustainability of the peg" falls and policy makers will face increasing pressure to realign the currency. This is true whether a financial crisis is imminent or not.

Events become more complicated during the run up before a collapse. This is because GAP will remain relatively small because the bandwagon keeps the free-market domestic currency value relatively high. Hence, governments can maintain a particular pegged value because market participants – for the time being – view it as reasonable. But tension is growing. The small GAP belies the fact that, based on the variables that currency market participants typically, but not currently, use to gauge the value of a currency (as indicated by the mental model forecast), it is seriously overvalued and teetering on the edge of an attack. The larger the

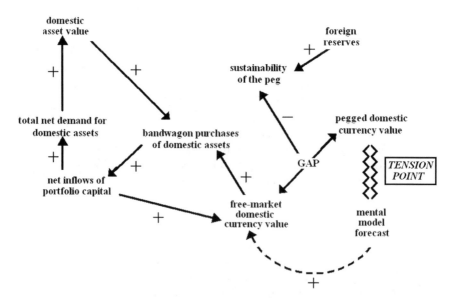

Figure 5.14 Currency crises: currency-forecast divergence under a fixed exchange rate regime.

difference between pegged domestic currency value and mental model forecast, the greater the pressure on the tension point, and the more mundane may be the event that leads agents to decide to take advantage of the situation and start the sell-off.

In either the flexible or fixed exchange rate scenario, the bandwagon effect is key. In the former, the tension accumulates as the domestic currency value moves above the mental model forecast; in the latter, it is the distance between the pegged domestic currency value (which can be maintained only because the bandwagon effect lends its support) and currency shadow forecast that is the issue. The greater the tension, the more likely a crisis occurs.

The next tension point to be explained will be that related to financial-returns divergence. It makes use of the domestic asset value cell already explained in Figures 5.13 and 5.14, but also considers the effect of the business cycle on physical investment. Chapter Twenty-two of Keynes' *General Theory* contains a summary of his view of the latter. While there are several important factors involved (see Harvey 2002b or Keller and Carlson 1982 for complete treatments), it is the relationship between the expectation of profit from investment and the existing stock of capital that guarantees downturns. Physical investment rules the roost in the domestic macroeconomy. If firms decide to invest less then, ceteris paribus, recession will result; if they decide to invest more, there will be an expansion. How they decide is, therefore, key, and an important determinant in their decision making is the effect of the existing stock of capital on the potential profits from investment. Simply put, the more capital already in existence, the less likely that adding to that stock will prove to be money-making. This is shown on Figure 5.15 in the link between stock of physical capital and π^e (the expectation of profit from investment variable from equation 5.5). Note the negative feedback loop that creates the business cycle: rising physical investment due to a high π^e will create economic expansion, but eventually the rise in the stock of physical capital will lower the expectation of profit from further investment sufficiently to cause physical investment to fall. This creates recession (the fact that agents' tend to overreact during both the upswing and downswing, is also key, but will not be modeled here – see Harvey 2002b and Keller and Carlson 1982). Eventually, π^e recovers and an expansion results (though it was Keynes' contention that the recovery process would take longer than the initial collapse). Thus, Figure 5.15 shows a basic business cycle.

The implication for crises is that, while bandwagon effects may cause financial returns (as shown by domestic asset values) to rise to unrealistic and unsustainable levels, real returns (π^e), though they may reach unreasonable levels for limited periods of time, are clearly anchored. Eventually, the saturated stock of capital will bring everyone back to earth. This should in turn lower financial returns commensurately since the two must ultimately be linked (hence the dashed line connecting them). However, there may be a considerable delay before this takes place. In fact, as expected physical and financial returns diverge, market participants may choose to channel funds into the asset market rather than real investment, thus exacerbating the situation by further bidding up asset prices (this

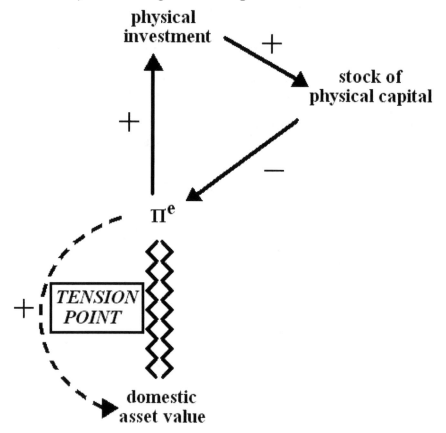

Figure 5.15 Currency crises: financial-returns divergence.

is not modeled explicitly). In this manner, the financial-returns divergence tension point created by the distance between π^e and domestic asset values grows more unstable. Eventually, the tension created by the fact that bandwagon-driven asset prices are continuing at a rate not justified by the expected and actual returns in the market for physical capital will cause a collapse in asset values. The greater the tension, the more commonplace may be the event that causes the rapid re-evaluation that leads to the crash.[16]

The last tension point is that related to financial fragility and it is based on Hyman Minsky's financial instability hypothesis (Minksy 1982, 1992, 1996). He argued that in a modern, capitalist economy, production takes time in the sense that some period must pass between the hiring of inputs and the sale of outputs. Firms must, therefore, finance both long-term investments like physical capital and the short-term costs associated with labor and raw materials. Consumers, too, take advantage of credit, and it is a function of the very nature of the business undertaken by banks and other financial institutions that they find themselves heavily indebted as they borrow short and loan long. These debts interlock as firms and consumers owe banks and banks owe firms, consumers, and other banks. The upshot of this interlock is that when one entity defaults it can, depending on the magnitudes involved, spread very quickly throughout the financial system.

Of course, if no one ever defaults, this is a non-issue. However, not only does default occur, but, because of the psychology of economic agents, such episodes tend to be concentrated in time and thus severe and potentially catastrophic. The core problem is the fact that how much debt agents consider to be "safe" varies systematically. Consider what happens during "good times," say an economic expansion or asset-market boom. Firms and consumers increase their spending, some of which is financed via loans. Banks happily extend the latter as they find themselves (having just emerged from "bad times) with plentiful excess reserves. This fuels the boom and, initially, firms, consumers, and financial institutions are all well satisfied by the ease with which loans are repaid. However, Minsky claims (consistent with the availability heuristic explained in Chapter Three) that economic agents have short memories and place far too much emphasis on the recent past as a indicator of future trends. Consequently, as the debt repayment schedule is met, all three groups decide that they had been too conservative in their estimates of how much could be financed with a given level income. Firms and consumers take on additional debt relative to income and banks allow them to do so. As this process continues, agents find themselves moving from hedge to speculative to Ponzi debt-income structures:

> Hedge financing units are those which can fulfill all of their contractual payment obligations by their cash flows: the greater the weight of equity financing in the liability structure, the greater the likelihood that the unit is a hedge financing unit. Speculative finance units are units that can meet their payment commitments on "income account" on their liabilities, even as they cannot repay the principle out of income cash flows. Such units need to "roll over" their liabilities: (e.g. issue new debt to meet commitments on maturing debt). Governments with floating debts, corporations with floating issues of commercial paper, and banks are typically hedge units.
>
> For Ponzi units, the cash flows from operations are not sufficient to fulfill either the repayment of principle or the interest due on outstanding debts by their cash flows from operations. Such units can sell assets or borrow. Borrowing to pay interest or selling assets to pay interest (and even dividends) on common stock lowers the equity of a unit, even as it increases liabilities and the prior commitment of future incomes.
>
> (Minsky 1992: 7)

Thus, as an economic expansion or asset-market boom continues, an increasing number of agents become speculative and then Ponzi units and the financial system become more and more prone to shocks. Inevitably, given the precarious position in which firms, consumers, and banks have placed themselves, defaults occur. This may happen because the expansion has petered out as the stock of capital has become saturated (as in Figure 5.15), the asset market boom has peaked, or simply because so many agents have moved toward the Ponzi-end of the continuum that even with appreciating assets and/or a growing economy, they could not meet their debt-repayment schedules. Depending on the level of interlock, agents' debt-to-income ratios, and the severity of the initial defaults, the debt deflation may be widespread or isolated. Once it is over, the remaining economically-viable agents revise downward the level of debt they believe they can manage with a given income. However, this conservatism does not last long. Once the bad memories have passed, the process of undermining the stability of the financial system starts all over again.

The lesson here is that agent behavior (in the absence of policies and institutions to control it) is such that it causes the financial system in capitalist economies to unravel at regular intervals. During good times, market participants become overly optimistic regarding expected returns, particularly financial ones. They repeatedly and predictably overextend themselves and their actions lead inevitably to disappointment and default in the financial sector.

While Minsky's theory was originally formulated in the context of a domestic business cycle, it can be extended to an open economy. A number of Post Keynesian authors have undertaken such a modification (Arestis and Glickman 2002, Cruz, Amann, and Walters 2006, Cypher 1996, Kregel 2004, Lopez 1998, and Wolfson 2002). An implicit understanding among these scholars has been that financial fragility is a much more serious issue when the economy involved is, a priori, weak and unstable. A financial collapse in a developed nation with high per-capita GDP, a relatively even distribution of income, and extensive social programs is unwelcome; it is an economic and social disaster in a developing nation.

Figure 5.16 presents Minsky's theory in an open-economy context. Recall that it is the ease of debt repayment that is key. As agents find that current income is sufficient to satisfy all commitments, so they decide to take on even more debt. As modeled here, that ease is directly related to two factors: π^e and domestic asset values. The former plays such a role for two reasons. First, as firms expect to earn more from physical investment, so they are willing to take on more debt and banks (sharing their enthusiasm) happily oblige. In addition, as π^e rises, so will physical investment and, therefore, national income (which, for simplicity, is not shown).

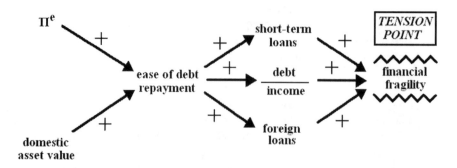

Figure 5.16 Currency crises: financial fragility.

This will encourage consumers as well as banks and firms. With respect to asset values, as they increase, those holding them feel wealthier (and borrow more) and it will serve as a positive reflection on the asset issuers (who may find loans offered at a discount).

So, either an upswing in the business cycle (via π^e) or an asset-market boom (via domestic asset values) will lead agents to lower their margins of safety and take on more debt per unit of income. The latter is shown directly on Figure 5.16 as debt/income, and this contributes to the financial fragility tension point as explained above. At the same time, agents' rising confidence tends to convince them that it is safe, despite the obvious risks, to finance an increasing percentage of their spending via short-term loans (see the corresponding cell on Figure 5.16). This creates what is known as "maturity mismatch," and the greater this becomes, the more prone to shocks the financial structure becomes (Grabel 2003: 320). Furthermore, in an open economy, it is not uncommon for agents' whose home currency is appreciating to borrow increasing amounts in now-cheap foreign monies (see "foreign loans" on Figure 5.16). Foreign investors rush to accommodate these demands, both via loans and through the equity market. As the level of "locational mismatch," or ratio of foreign currency indebtedness to total indebtedness, increases, lenders and borrowers find themselves more and more vulnerable to a sudden currency depreciation or devaluation (Grabel 2003: 320). In sum, locational and maturity mismatch combine with a rising debt-to-income ratio to create an increasingly unstable financial structure. Each of these occurs because agents overestimate their ability to service debt.

Figure 5.17 combines the processes that create the individual tension points (and 5.18 does the same for a fixed exchange rate regime). Three feedback loops are modeled: "π^e-physical investment-stock of physical capital," "net inflows of portfolio capital-total net demand for domestic assets-domestic asset values-bandwagon purchases of domestic assets," and "net inflows of portfolio capital-domestic currency value-bandwagon purchases of domestic assets." The first is negative while the last two are positive and share two cells. In considering a typical scenario, financial liberalization policies in a developing state may cause a jump in domestic and foreign demand for domestic assets. This sets into motion the two positive feedback loops, meaning that domestic asset values and the value of the currency are now on steep, upward slopes. This gives domestic confidence a boost, possibly (though this is not explicitly modeled) raising π^e along with the asset values. This increases the ease of debt repayment and agents start increasing debt/income and the ratio of short-term and foreign loans.

All three tension points are now coming into play. Financial fragility is increasing as agents raise short-term loans, debt/income, and foreign loans; currency values are rising out of line with what the mental model forecast would have justified, and, inevitably, the rate of return on financial assets will rise well out of line with those associated with real returns (as the stock of capital is saturated and causes a fall or at least deceleration in π^e). It does not really matter where the tension causes a break first. Whether it is the currency-price divergence, financial-returns divergence, or financial-fragility point, once the day of reckoning arises, any

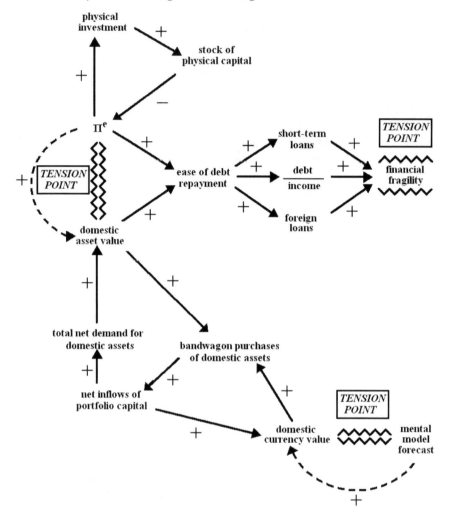

Figure 5.17 Currency crises: complete system with three tension points under a flexible exchange rate regime.

negativity in one will quickly spread to one or both of the others as agents panic and a crisis results. Currency and asset values and physical and financial investment will all collapse.

A SHORT LOOK AT LONG-RUN EXCHANGE RATE MOVEMENTS

Neoclassical economics draws an important distinction between short-run and long-run phenomena. Generally speaking, they see the long run as characterized by fewer constraints, rigidities, and transaction costs and more closely matching

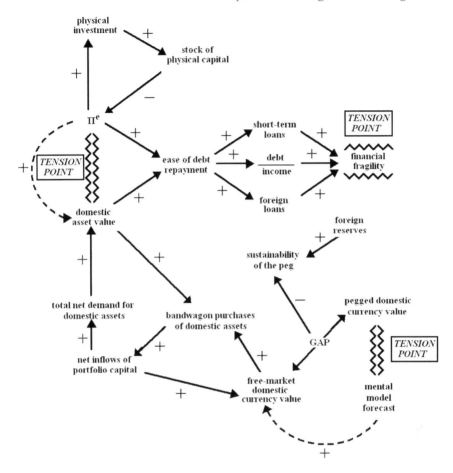

Figure 5.18 Currency crises: complete system with three tension points under a fixed exchange rate regime.

the outcomes predicted by their theories (i.e., full employment and Pareto-optimal equilibria). Post Keynesian economists (particularly of the Keynes variety, as opposed to the Ricardian/Kaleckian branch) have never seen this as a particularly useful approach and in fact tend to view the Neoclassical use of the long run simply as a means for those economists to assume away the real world issues that make their premises most difficult to justify.

Because Post Keynesians emphasize historical time and path dependence, they see the long run as simply the aggregation of short runs. The state of the world today is a function of all the various events that shaped it yesterday. The fact that the Great Depression occurred means that the environment in which economic activity takes place today is different than it would have been had the Depression never happened. The Asian crisis in 1997 shunted economic activity onto a new track and means that where they are now is a direct result of that. There are of course some phenomena that simply create white noise around a trend (the cash-in effect, for example) and some that are more frequent or important than others when viewed from a distance. But we cannot simply assume that the impact of short-term phenomena averages out to zero, nor can we necessarily identify the frequent or important variables a priori. Circumstances may require that we try to do so on occasion, but in general there is, as Keynes pointed out, only one time horizon over which economic activity is logically understood. This point is absolutely critical to understanding the Post Keynesian view of exchange rate determination.

CONCLUSIONS

Taken together, the open-economy, Z-D diagram and the mental-model schematic offer a Post Keynesian view of exchange rate determination. The latter paints a picture of a world where agents actively search for information to input into their evolving view of the currency market, using the signals generated there to inform their portfolio management decisions. One can then lift the $/FX Forecast from that model and use it to position FXM in the upper-left quadrant of the open-economy Z-D diagram, which then shows currency prices in the broader context of the macroeconomy. There is no expectation that exchange rate movements will encourage either balanced trade or full employment. In addition, it is probable that currency prices will be volatile and prone – particularly in developing countries – to crisis. The means by which the latter may take place is complex and interwoven with other factors and thus requires a separate analysis, as shown in Figures 5.17 and 5.18. There, it is shown that, as a matter of course, agent behavior creates unsustainable processes which may cause massive booms and equally massive collapses. Such events may not take place on a daily basis, but we should not be surprised when they do.

What can be done to protect ourselves from all this will be covered in Chapter Seven. In the meantime, chapter six uses the models developed here to explain the post-Bretton Woods dollar and the Asian and Mexican financial crises.

6 Real-world applications

The previous three chapters have focused on establishing basic facts about exchange rates and building models to explain currency price determination. It has been argued that, first and foremost, financial capital flows play the dominant role in today's market (in both the short and long run). Those flows are in turn a function of agents' potentially volatile expectations as guided by their mental model, which is related but not inevitably bound to what might be traditionally called "fundamental" factors. Psychological influences such as bandwagon effects and forecast-construction bias may also affect market participants' forecast. That crises emerge is a function of the means by which exchange rates are determined, plus agents' overly optimistic expectations of both profit and the level of debt they can safely carry.

In this chapter, the models developed in the previous one are used to explain the post-Bretton Woods history of the dollar (*vis-à-vis* the Deutsche Mark and, after December 1998, the euro) and the Mexican and Asian financial crises.[1] For the former, the events are outlined and then shown exactly as they would appear on the augmented mental model and open-economy Z-D diagram. In general, we should expect to see currency prices moved by bandwagon effects, interest rate differentials (especially as we move beyond Bretton Woods and capital flows increase in size), macro growth and stability (sometimes as indicated by unemployment rates), inflation, and trade imbalances (though the last only sporadically). When explaining the crises, they are described in the context of the schematic developed at the end of Chapter Five. It is expected that data will show that catastrophic depreciations occur when financial returns far outstrip real ones, agents take on unsustainable levels of debt, and currency prices become separated from the predictions of the mental model.

As mentioned earlier, Post Keynesians do not assume that economic modeling creates a black box into which we can place inputs that then generate deterministic predictions or explanations. These models are to be used as a means of guiding the analysis rather than ruling it. They suggest those phenomena most likely to play an important role in currency price determination and crises, but other factors may be important, too. For that reason, to truly understand the Post Keynesian analyses of exchange rates and crises, they must be seen in the context of an explanation of real-world events.

THE POST-BRETTON WOODS HISTORY OF THE DOLLAR

In the discussion that follows, the dollar's fortunes are measured with respect to the Deutsche Mark and, once that disappeared, the euro. Roughly speaking, each period identified represents a long-term rise or fall in the value of the dollar. Given that, the post-Bretton Woods era can be divided into six episodes: Bretton Woods Collapse and Adjustment (1971–79), Dollar Run Up (1980–85), Dollar Reversal (1985–95), Last Days of the Mark (1995–98), Euro Decline (1999–2001), and Euro Recovery (2001–08). The highlights of each, along with the driving factors, follow.

Bretton Woods collapse and adjustment: 1971 to 1979

The period from the end of the fixed exchange rate system through the second OPEC oil embargo witnessed a sustained decline in the dollar (see Figure 6.1). This began under Bretton Woods as payment imbalances weighed against the US and led to several dollar devaluations. As capital flows grew and the absolute size of speculative money in the portfolio capital market increased, so it became more and more difficult for governments to defend par rates. In the end, the pressure from speculators (who were betting on further and/or larger dollar devaluations than were forthcoming) was such that the US decided to allow the dollar to float. The dollar experienced a brief rebound as its trade account moved into surplus (around 1973–74), but that surplus turned generally into a growing deficit (with a brief

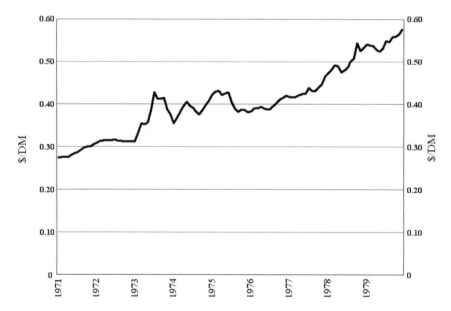

Figure 6.1 $/FX during the Bretton Woods Collapse and Adjustment, 1971–79 (Federal Reserve Bank of New York data).

interruption in 1975) for the rest of the period. The value of the dollar followed as agents took this as a sign of a continuation of the weak US economic performance that had led to the collapse of Bretton Woods. In addition, US inflation stayed mostly above the German and the gap between US and German unemployment, though closing, favored Germany throughout the period. It is also likely that the dollar carried with it some negative bandwagon and sentiment because of its public role in the collapse of Bretton Woods. As evidence of this possibility, US interest rates and industrial production actually rose with respect to the German through this period. However, such was market participants' tendency to interpret dollar news in a bad light that this was actually one of the few times in the post-Bretton Woods era that rising US macro growth was seen as a negative given its potential to raise US imports.

This is shown on Figures 6.2 and 6.3. In the former, agents' interpretation of events is highlighted and, for clarity, those lines of causation that did not play an important role are omitted. This convention is followed throughout the chapter. In addition, notes and variables are added where necessary, with the latter treated as members of the set "Indicators" (though not placed physically inside the oval). The following discussion will repeat some of the above, but the intent is to show exactly how the events described in the previous paragraph are illustrated in the model. In the sections that follow, I will dispense with the introductory description and jump straight to reconciling the historical events with the model.

Most important in this period was the negative medium-term expectation and accompanying bandwagon the dollar carried with it from the collapse of Bretton Woods (shown in the medium-term expectations box and the positive feedback loop on the far right). While the latter had the effect of directly contributing to net PFI_{us} outflows and dollar depreciation, the former led agents to ignore otherwise positive US developments and overweight negative ones (see, for example, the notation on expected interest rate differentials). Because of this, not only was the primary focus through this period on US trade imbalances (which were not, paradoxically, consistently poor, though they had turned to deficit by the end of the period), this

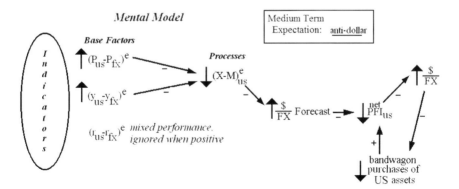

Figure 6.2 Augmented mental model during the Bretton Woods Collapse and Adjustment, 1971–79.

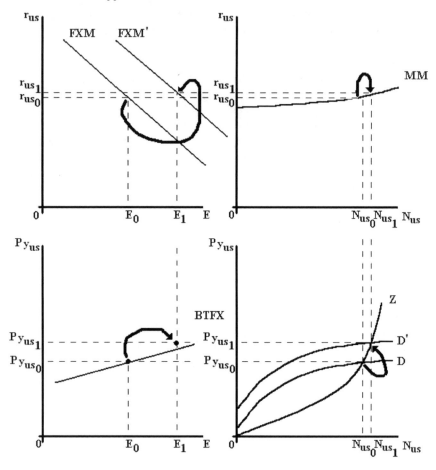

Figure 6.3 Open-economy Z-D during the Bretton Woods Collapse and Adjustment,
1971–79.

was one of the few times that agents took a superior US macro performance to be
indicative of a future depreciation since it would encourage imports (hence the
existence of only one line of causation from $(y_{us} - y_{fx})^e$, which leads to trade flows
and not financial capital). The entire period represents a sort of mini collapse of
the dollar wherein the fall of Bretton Woods (along with other dramatic events like
Watergate) gave the US currency significant downward momentum and pushed
it past what agents might have considered appropriate based on the mental model
alone. In fact, the overshooting was such that when recovery came, it was in the
form of an equally dramatic rebound.

In terms of the open-economy Z-D diagram, the key piece of information
to transfer from Figure 6.2 is, of course, the fall in the forecast value of the
dollar (illustrated by the rightward shift of FXM). The US economy generally
performed well and interest rate movements favored the dollar. For these reasons,

D is shifted upward and this creates pressure on MM that leads r_{us} to move from r_{us0} to r_{us1}. Meanwhile, the US trade account went from rough balance to deficit, despite the dollar depreciation. Note that the flat BTFX curve is able to show this development.

Dollar run up: 1980 through February 1985

At the very end of the above period a regime change took place that led to a major revision in the indicators included in agents' mental model (see Figure 6.4 for the dollar's movements). First, central banks throughout the developed world adopted a strong stance against inflation, using monetary policy as their primary tool. Second, in October of 1979, the Federal Reserve announced a shift to targeting of monetary aggregates rather than interest rates.[2] Meanwhile, Monetarism had become a very popular perspective among academic economists. The combination of these events not only caused US interest rates to rise to historic levels, but it led agents to include rates of money supply growth in the set of indicators and to interpret inflation as a sign that real interest rates in that country would soon rise. This is why $(P_{us} - P_{fx})^e$ is not shown in its traditional role in Figure 6.5. Instead, it is to be understood that information regarding relative inflation is entering the mental model as an indicator and then through the link labeled "US monetary policy shift" and into interest rate expectations. In general, as market participants had became jaded by the size and resilience of the US trade deficit (which is shown as "ignored" in Figure 6.5), they began to look instead at variables more closely

Figure 6.4 $/FX during the Dollar Run Up, 1980–5 (Federal Reserve Bank of New York data).

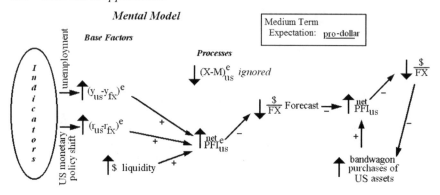

Figure 6.5 Augmented mental model during the Dollar Run Up, 1980–85.

related to portfolio capital investment, particularly interest rates. The latter were the primary driving force throughout this period, though there was also a move to the dollar as safe haven (see the increase in dollar liquidity on Figure 6.5) in light of world unrest (Cumby 1988). It is noteworthy that even when the pro-US interest differential closed in the fall of 1984, momentum continued to push the dollar over the last five or six months, a sign that the market was in a boom period where the medium-term expectations and the bandwagon effect became the primary drivers of the currency price. Relative inflation was very mixed while German unemployment, which started at less than one-half the US rate, rose almost to equality by the end (hence the up arrow on $(y_{us} - y_{fx})^e$, despite the deep recession in the United States – note, too, that it was unemployment that agents used as their primary indicator of macro health during this period, as indicated).

There are three salient events on the open-economy Z-D: the change in the monetary policy stance leading to the upward shift of MM and a rise in r_{us}; the shift and movement along FXM (the former as a function of decreases in the $/FX Forecast shown on Figure 6.5), and the large increase in the US trade deficit. While the US experienced a severe recession during this period, it was followed by a strong recovery. I therefore chose to leave Z and D in Figure 6.6 unchanged, though I suspect that one could make an argument for lowering D. In that event, one must still show a net rise in r_{us} and the US trade deficit and a fall in $/FX.

Dollar reversal: March 1985 through April 1995

The bust arrived quickly thereafter (see Figure 6.7). When the bandwagon effect moves the exchange rate well out of line with the price expected by relying solely on the mental model, then the confidence of agents in subsequent forecasts may decline. The more tenuous the foundation, the less it takes to shatter it and start a rush in the opposite direction (just as in a currency crisis). Such a development is especially likely when a particularly dramatic episode had been the impetus for the currency run (e.g., a change in Federal Reserve policy and a sharp rise in the dollar interest rate).

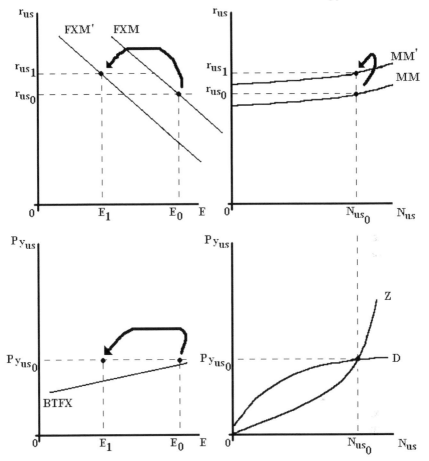

Figure 6.6 Open-economy Z-D during the Dollar Run Up, 1980–85.

Hence, in spring of 1985, when the dollar had peaked and agents were becoming increasingly anxious regarding the likelihood of depreciation (especially in light of the fact that the dollar advantage in the interest rate differential had been closing for some months), the fact that data were suggesting a weaker US economy was taken as the cue to begin the rapid slide. When officials in the United States, Germany, Britain, Japan, and France announced in September that they would pursue an "orderly" dollar depreciation, this only aggravated the situation (as did a sudden concern with the US "twin deficits" of trade and federal budget which was encouraged by the attention paid by the scholarly and popular press – note that these are shown as "Plaza Accord" and "Twin Deficits" indicators contributing to the expectation of a fall in net expected PFI_{us}). The superior inflation performance of the US over the first half of this period was largely ignored (if not interpreted as a negative, indicating low future interest rates). Likewise, the generally better unemployment numbers in the US did little to affect the dollar (both are indicated

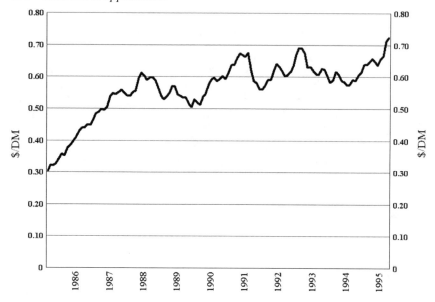

Figure 6.7 $/FX during the Dollar Reversal, 1985–95 (Federal Reserve Bank of New York data).

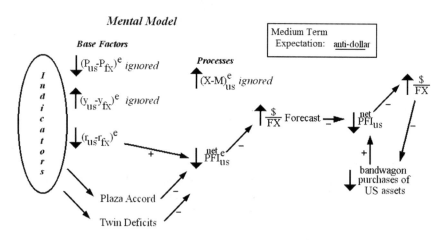

Figure 6.8 Augmented mental model during the Dollar Reversal, 1985–95.

by "ignored" labels on Figure 6.8). By 1987, the dollar had fallen below even its post-Bretton Woods collapse level. Within eight years (1980–87) the dollar had almost doubled and then halved (versus the mark). It is very difficult to imagine how one could justify this as a function of the underlying "fundamentals."

From 1987 through 1995, the dollar moved generally lower but in very mixed trading. This appears to have been largely due to the persistent negative interest rate differential between the dollar and the mark. It is also likely that the precipitous drop had created a negative medium-term expectation and bandwagon for the dollar. Trade flows had little impact through most of this period as the US deficit generally improved (at least during the first half of the period when the US experienced sluggish growth and recession); the dollar continued to fall (note the "ignored" label on trade flows). Only at the end (beginning in 1994) does the reversal in the current account appear to be correlated with a move in the dollar.

Most important to indicate on Z-D in Figure 6.9 are the fall in dollar interest rates (note the downward shift in MM), the strong rise in $/FX Forecast (leading to the rightward shift in FXM), and the improvement in the trade balance (see the BTFX diagram). Again, for simplicity, I chose not to shift anything on Z-D, but a rise in D could have been justified (with the caveat that the net directions of change in the MM, FXM, and BTFX diagrams must remain the same).

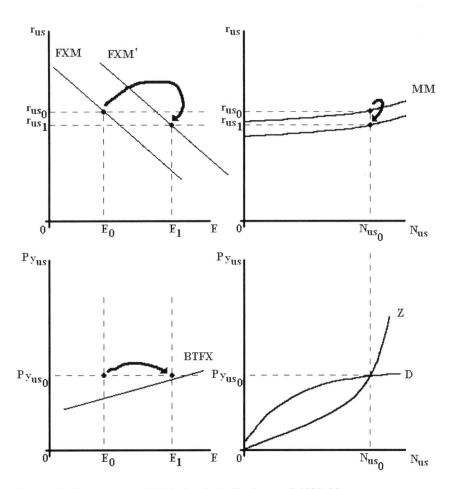

Figure 6.9 Open-economy Z-D during the Dollar Reversal, 1985–95.

Last days of the mark: 1995 through 1998

Though US inflation performance versus Germany was generally inferior during this period, the dollar rallied in early 1995 and continued to do so almost continuously (save a minor reversal that started in August of 1997) through the last days of the mark (note that $(P_{us} - P_{fx})^e$ is marked "ignored" on Figure 6.11; Figure 6.10 shows dollar movements over this period). That it did was due almost entirely to interest differentials, which had turned positive and remained there. Meanwhile, as macro data became available, the tendency was to decide how this might impact

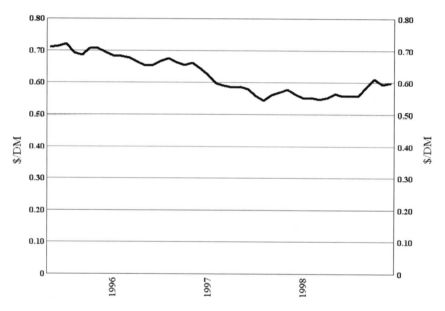

Figure 6.10 $/FX during the Last Days of the Mark, 1995–98 (Federal Reserve Bank of New York data).

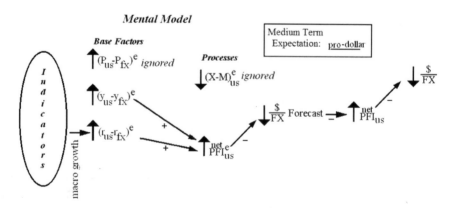

Figure 6.11 Augmented mental model during the Last Days of the Mark, 1995–98.

interest rate policy in the country in question: strong growth was thought to suggest tight monetary policy, and weak the opposite. Indeed, on average (up to the last few months), such data (e.g., unemployment) generally favored the US against Germany. Interestingly, the collapse of US net exports was almost entirely ignored. Figure 6.11 shows the dominant role of interest rate differentials, including the unusual role played by macro growth in this period (noted by the addition of "macro growth" as an indicator affecting relative interest rates) and the market's decision to ignore inflation and trade flows. Bandwagon effects did not appear to play a strong role in this period, though there was clear pro-dollar sentiment over the medium term.

Figure 6.12 shows the strong US economic expansion (upward shift in D) along with tighter monetary policy (upward shift in MM), and expectations of a stronger dollar (leftward shift in FXM). This all combined to create a large and growing trade deficit in the US, as shown in the BTFX quadrant.

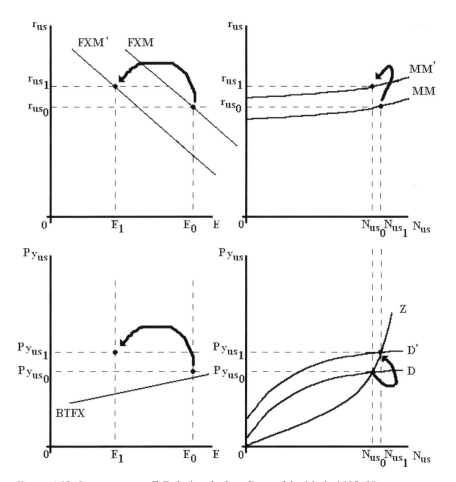

Figure 6.12 Open-economy Z-D during the Last Days of the Mark, 1995–98.

Euro's decline: 1999 through June 2001

Though the mark ceased to exist and the euro was born in January 1999, the beginning of the next period is really a continuation of the previous one (see Figure 6.13). The primary factor imparting the downward momentum (and a bandwagon) was simply the interest rate differential. So long as it remained positive with respect to the dollar, the euro fell. In addition, there was concern rather than euphoria regarding the new monetary instrument and thus capital began to flow out of Europe (the latter indicated by the negative impact of "Advent of the Euro" on Figure 6.14).

The interest rate differential that had given the mark and then the euro downward momentum began to close in mid-1999, and did so by 2001. Still, the euro fell, now more on momentum than economic indicators. Indeed, though the trends were unclear at the time, US inflation and macro performance (marked with "ignored" on Figure 6.14) were generally worse than German.[3] Market participants expressed some confusion over this themselves, suggesting that the bandwagon factors may well have taken over from the mental model as shown in Figure 5.13. The euro had lost roughly 35 percent of its value in 30 months, numbers very difficult to justify in fundamental terms (and especially given that it was about to rocket in the other direction). Though the dollar's rise in this period was perhaps not as dramatic as that experienced through 1985, the conditions were similar: a general background of profitable interest rate differentials were coupled with a dramatic event in the political/economic arena. And again, as in 1985, an equally dramatic reversal was in the offing.

Figure 6.13 $/FX during the Euro Decline, 1999–2001 (Federal Reserve Bank of New York data).

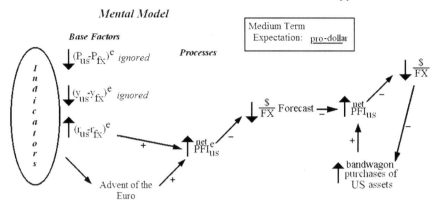

Figure 6.14 Augmented mental model during the Euro Decline, 1999–2001.

In the Z-D diagram (Figure 6.15), you see evidence of the fall in \$/FX Forecast from Figure 6.14 and a dramatic rise in the already large US trade deficit. Monetary policy is shown as tightening so that interest rates rise but, again I chose not to complicate the diagram by shifting Z or D. In this instance, had I done so it might have been appropriate to shift D upward (though this period ends with a US recession), which would have magnified the rise in the trade deficit and interest rates.

Euro recovery: July 2001 through 2008

Interest rate differentials had already become negative with respect to the dollar by April of 2001, though the dollar continued to appreciate through June. Thereafter and through 2008, interest paid on the euro exceeded that on the dollar in comparable accounts – and the euro rapidly made up for lost ground (see Figure 6.16). Comparatively little attention was paid to inflation (which was generally higher and rising in the US – this is marked "ignored" on Figure 6.17) and unemployment (note the question mark in front of $(y_{us} - y_{fx})^e$, indicating that indicators of US versus foreign growth were mixed, and largely ignored in any event). A new variable (re)entered the scene, however: the US trade balance. Its appearance was, indeed, spectacular, with the trade deficit more than doubling in nominal terms by the close of 2005. At the time of this writing (May 2008), there has been a slight recovery in the current account balance, but the dollar is floundering at historic lows. Meanwhile, markets are concerned with the viability of the US financial sector due to the latter's involvement with subprime lending (i.e., lending to agents with a high default risk) and the news regarding the US macroeconomy remains mixed so that there appears to be little hope that US interest rates will rise in the near future. However, once the dollar does pick up, it would not be surprising to find that it does so rapidly.

Figure 6.18 has the open-economy Z-D for this period. It shows the decline in US interest rates (downward shift in MM), the currency-market preference for the euro over the dollar (rightward shift in FXM), and the rising trade deficit. Note that

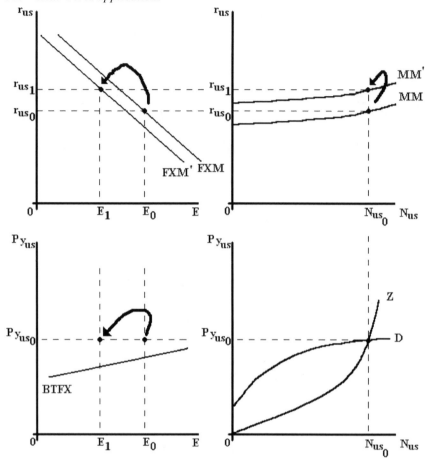

Figure 6.15 Open-economy Z-D during the Euro Decline, 1999–2001.

the last occurred despite a falling dollar and a largely stagnant US macroeconomy. This is so because, as Robert Scott has calculated, "Rapid increases in the price of oil and related products were responsible for 63 percent of the increase in the deficit" (Scott 2006). In other words, a rise in the price of imports combined with price inelasticity of demand caused a rightward shift in BTFX that was sufficiently large to more than offset the dollar depreciation. The current account has improved over the past several months, but thus far this has been minor compared to the initial deterioration.

CURRENCY CRISES

As suggested in Chapter Five, international financial crises can be explained in the context of the three tension points illustrated in Figures 5.17 (for flexible exchange

Figure 6.16 $/FX during the Euro Recovery, 2001–08 (Federal Reserve Bank of New York data).

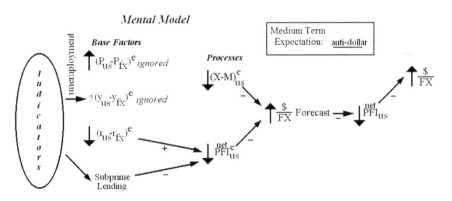

Figure 6.17 Augmented mental model during the Euro Recovery, 2001–08.

rate systems) and 5.18 (for fixed). These are a function of bandwagon effects in currency and asset markets, a Keynes'-style business cycle, and the tendency of agents to take on increasing levels of debt during "good times." Study of real-world currency crises should show evidence of agents bidding up (or holding) currency values above those levels implied by the mental model, excessive financial rates of return, and increasing financial fragility. Eventually, one of these untenable processes will reach the breaking point and a catastrophic deflation will result.

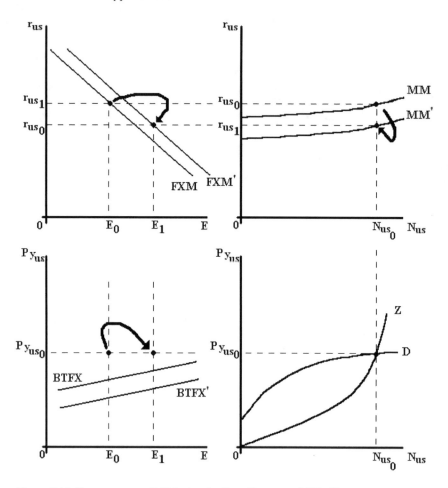

Figure 6.18 Open-economy Z-D during the Euro Recovery, 2001–08.

The Mexican financial crisis: 1994

Two recent and particularly dramatic examples of this phenomenon were the Mexican and Asian financial crises. Beginning with the former, it occurred in 1994 and led not only to the collapse of the peso, but a 6 percent contraction in real GDP. While the immediate cause appears to have been comments from President Ernesto Zedillo regarding the possible need to devalue the peso (called "The December Mistake" by outgoing president Carlos Salinas), the seeds were sown in the 1980s.

In order to understand what happened, recall Figure 5.18 (which will be used because the peso was on a sliding peg). As is not uncommon in developing-country crises, the catalyst appears to have come from a policy shock. In fact, a series of financial liberalization measures were put in place (see for example Cruz, Amann, and Walters 2006). As Julio Lopez-Gallardo, Juan Carlos Moreno-Brid, and Martin Puchet Anyul explain:

The first step was the implementation of a system of auctions, whereby the interest rates were established for commercial bank deposits at the central bank and lending from the central to commercial banks. Later on, in the second half of the 1980s, the mandatory reserve ratio of banks was drastically reduced (from 50 per cent to 10 per cent) and the interest rates for some specific banking instruments were liberalized. In turn, commercial banks were given complete freedom to allocate according to their own preferences the resources obtained from these instruments. This reform was followed by the full and complete liberalization of domestic interest rates in 1988. The banking system was re-privatized in 1990, and a year later the mandatory reserve ratio was eliminated for all banking liabilities denominated in domestic currency. In 1993 commercial banking portfolio investment was completely deregulated.
(Lopez-Gallardo, Moreno-Brid, and Anyul 2006: 370)

Ilene Grabel adds, "The attraction of large inflows of [portfolio investment] after 1989 resulted from the Brady Plan-proscribed neoliberal reforms" (Grabel 1996: 447).

The intent of these measures was, of course, to open up financial markets and thereby attract the capital necessary for real economic growth. What happened instead was that while the policies encouraged domestic and foreign demand for Mexican financial assets (via net demand for domestic assets and net inflows of portfolio capital on Figure 5.18), real growth lagged considerably. The two positive feedback loops on the bottom portion of the diagram were soon working to drive up financial asset values and support what might otherwise have been considered an overvalued peso. As evidence of the former, from 1989 to 1994, real (deflated by CPI) share prices rose at an annual rate of 33.1 percent; during that same period, real GDP growth was 3.91 percent – not paltry, but well below what agents in the financial market were expecting to earn (International Monetary Fund CD-Rom). Tension was thus clearly growing at the financial-returns divergence point on the left-hand side of the diagram. There was, in addition, a general shift in economic activity as, from 1980 to 1993, GDP represented by industry fell from 22 percent to 20 percent, while that comprised of finance and real estate went from 8.6 percent to 14.9 percent (Cypher 1996: 452).

With respect to the peso, the booming asset market was allowing the government to maintain the pegged rate. It did this by keeping GAP small due to the bandwagon effect (see Figure 5.18). This merely delays the inevitable, of course, and tends to make the day of reckoning much more serious once it does arrive. Unfortunately, it is not really possible to prove that market participants would have, under other circumstances, believed that the peso was overvalued. However, we do know that the real value of the peso in dollars actually climbed 4.64 percent per year from 1986 to 1994, and that this occurred despite the fact that Mexican real GDP growth lagged behind US and the Mexican current account went from modest surplus in

1987 to a $30 billion deficit in 1994 (the US experienced a substantial improvement in their trade balance; all data from International Monetary Fund CD-Rom). Of the tangible variables on the mental model, only the interest-rate differential favored the peso. Though this is generally a very important determinant of exchange rate movements, the fact that tension was growing everywhere else in the system meant that it would soon prove to be insufficient to generate a mental-model forecast that remained reasonably close to the pegged domestic currency value. The currency-forecast divergence point was thus growing increasingly strained. One more indication of the weakening position of the peso was the fact that the ratio of foreign currency reserves to the current-account deficit (a commonly used indicator of the ability of a nation to maintain a fixed rate – the numerator appears on Figure 5.18) fell from 206 percent in 1988 to 21 percent in 1994 (International Monetary Fund CD-Rom). These all contributed to the rapid exit from peso-denominated assets that followed the December Mistake.

This leaves financial fragility to be examined. Given the growing real economy and the asset-market boom, Figure 5.18 would predict a rise in debt/income, particularly short-term and foreign-denominated. These certainly occurred in Mexico leading up to the crisis. According to Cruz, Amann, and Walters (2006), domestic credit to the private sector rose from 11 percent of GDP in 1988 to 39 percent in 1994. And in terms of locational mismatch, Lopez-Gallardo, Moreno-Brid, and Anyul indicate that "… the inflow of foreign funds resulted in heavy external indebtedness of the private sector, including the banks; the exposure of the latter in foreign currency rose from about 19,000 (million of dollars) in December 1992, to about 24,000 in December 1993, and to 25,000 in December 1994" (Lopez-Gallardo, Moreno-Brid, and Anyul 2006: 376). On that same subject, Cypher writes, "By late 1994, the OECD estimated that one-third of the loans extended by the Mexican banks were in foreign currencies and that 25 percent of these loans were to businesses and individuals who had no income in foreign currencies" (Cypher 1996: 456). In other words, debtors in Mexico were becoming more and more dependent on the value of the peso remaining where it was. The data on maturity mismatch are a little more mixed in that there was actually a decline in short-term borrowing from 1990 to 1992; but there was then a rapid reversal such that it increased sharply up through the crisis (Cruz, Amann, and Walters 2006:715, Figure 3). All these developments were, not surprisingly, accompanied by a rise in non-performing loans, which were "estimated to be more than double the value of the equity capital of the entire Mexican banking system by late 1995" (Cypher 1996: 457). This is wholly consistent with Minksy's hypothesis.

The above offers evidence of increasing tension at all three points in Figure 5.18. The seeds of the crisis were sown by free-market reforms dating back to the 1980s and continuing up through the early 1990s. These caused a bidding up of asset prices, which led to unrealistic expectations of returns in the financial sector, debt-burdened economic agents whose liabilities were weighted toward the short-term and foreign currency, and a willingness to peg the peso at a level well above what the market could sustain. That the first inklings of a problem arose from comments about the currency peg is not really significant. In the end, so long as the processes contributing to the three tension points continued, one of them was going to break and the rapid outflow of portfolio capital (and collapse of asset and currency values) would have followed.

The Asian financial crisis: 1997

The story of the Asian financial crisis parallels that of Mexico's in terms of a Minsky-style run up in debt levels and bandwagon-supported pegged currency values; however, rather than the financial-returns divergence point emerging in the stock-market, it did so in real estate. As Thailand's experience was not only typical, but the first in the row of dominoes, this analysis will trace their experience.[4]

From 1985 to 1995, Thailand's was the fastest growing economy in the world (Jackson 1999: 172). According to the World Bank's *East Asian Miracle Report*, it was a model for economic development (Lauridsen 1998: 137). But, from June 1997 to July 1998, Thai GDP fell from 170 billion to 102 billion US dollars (Jackson 1999: 2). Mired in the worst economic crisis of their history, one had to ask how this could have happened to an economy with such a strong endorsement from the world's economics establishment.

Again, Figure 5.18 should be employed rather than 5.17 as the Thai baht was pegged to the dollar. And again, we can point to a series of neo-liberal reforms as the seeds of the disaster. Pasuk Phongpaichit and Chris Baker write that:

> From the mid-1980s, there was a rapid sequence of policy changes: conversion to export of manufactures, increased openness to foreign investment, and liberalization of the capital market … From 1989 to 1993, Thailand pursued financial liberalization including capital account convertibility, stock market reforms, and the creation of an offshore banking facility.
>
> (Phongpaichit and Baker 2004: 151)

These reforms had, as they did in Mexico, the effect of rapidly raising expectations to unrealistic levels. Joseph Lim cites data that show the ratio of portfolio investment inflows to GDP in Thailand rising from 0.25 in 1981–85 to 0.94 in 1986–89 to 1.42 in 1990–94 (Lim 2004: 50). By 1996, this ratio was 2.43 (Lim 2004: 50). Based on Figure 5.18, one would expect this to drive financial returns higher. It did, but not in the stock market. In terms of the latter, although from 1993 to 1994 real GDP grew at 8.6 percent per while CPI-deflated stock prices rose by 23.3 percent per year, Thai stock prices were actually declining the two years before the crisis. At the same time, however, there was a rise in the percentage of GDP associated with finance, which went from 4.6 percent in 1989 to 10.5 percent in 1996 (author's calculations, data from Asian Development Bank) and in Bangkok, new housing construction increased by an average of 17 percent per year while land prices quintupled in the central business district and rose by over 3000 percent in outer areas (real estate data are for 1987 to 1995; Sheng and Kirinpanu 2000: 14). By contrast, rates of real GDP growth were declining and in 1996 it appeared that this trend was accelerating (Lauridsen 1998: 143). The financial-returns divergence point was becoming tense.

Meanwhile, there were concerns about the fact that the baht was being pulled higher by the rising dollar to which it was pegged, but no immediate action was taken (Lauridsen 1998: 144). Capital was still flowing in, which made it unnecessary for Thai authorities to buy their own currency to keep it at the fixed rate since portfolio investors were doing it for them. But, Thai growth was rapidly slowing and its current account deficit was ballooning. And while the collapse in the ratio of foreign-currency reserves to the current-account deficit was not as pronounced as in Mexico, it had fallen from 378 percent in 1993 to 253 percent in 1996. Market participants were clearly aware of the currency-forecast divergence as attacks were made on the baht as early as November and December of 1996 (Lauridsen 1998: 145).

With respect to financial fragility, the rising real-estate prices and relatively high if shrinking growth rates caused agents' margins of safety to do precisely what Minsky's theory predicts they would do in good economic times. Measured as a percent of long-term debt, the short-term debt load doubled from 1981–85 to 1996 (author's calculations using data from Lim 2004: 50) and external debt rose from 36.06 percent of GDP in 1981–85 to 49.94 percent in 1996 (Lim 2004: 50). Hence, both maturity and locational mismatch was rising. Against this, because physical investment opportunities were drying up, not only did this mean that recession loomed, but those caught up in the cycle of increasing debt loads were funneling their newly borrowed funds into increasingly speculative ventures. As Yap Koie Sheng and Sakchai Kirinpanu write, "It would not be an exaggeration to say that half of Bangkok's landed families became real estate developers and the other half became real estate investors and speculators" (Sheng and Kirinpanu 2000: 15). They later add, "Many developers had one characteristic in common: they did very little market research which was considered unnecessary, because the demand was everywhere" (Sheng and Kirinpanu 2000: 15). According to the theory of crises put forth in the previous chapter, they were bound to be disappointed.

And so, at a time when the baht was being supported by a tenuous bandwagon and Thais were locked into short-term and foreign debt, the first cracks emerged in the housing market. This actually occurred in waves, with the first striking in 1994. But the problems became most evident after the release of a government report in 1997 (note the additional evidence of initial overconfidence and locational mismatch in the description):

> The news of an enormous oversupply of housing pushed speculators to dump their units. This further subdued housing prices and made it more difficult for developers to sell their units. This shifted attention to the situation of the developers. As the economy slowed down and interest rate increased, it became harder to sell units, while buyers stopped making down payments. Once it was clear that many developers were in trouble, the attention shifted to financial institutions. Developers had heavily borrowed from banks and finance companies, with large developers borrowing on offshore markets. Without

repayments by the developers, the finance companies became insolvent, but this was not immediately clear to the general public.

(Sheng and Kirinpanu 2000: 18)

They soon did learn, however, when Somprasong Land defaulted on their Eurobond interest payment in February 1997 (Lauridsen 1998: 147). This led to further revelations regarding the unsound state of the Thai financial market (caused by unrealistic expectations in the real estate market combined with locational and maturity mismatch), reversing the capital outflows that had heretofore made it possible to support the baht peg. By mid-year, authorities were forced to allow the baht to float and its collapse followed thereafter.

CONCLUSIONS

Post Keynesians build models that are intended to be explanations of the real world and not academic thought experiments. They therefore see testing their predictions against the facts of experience as a vital step in the process of model development. This chapter's history of the movement of the dollar since the end of Bretton Woods and of the Mexican and Asian financial crises shows that an explanation based on Post Keynesian principles can succeed in showing what has driven exchange rates in this era of large portfolio capital flows.[5] This is terribly important and encouraging and means that, with the models so vetted, the next chapter can consider policy.

7   Problems and policy

Economics is ultimately about policy. Though we inevitably spend most of our time and effort in trying to understand the causal processes at work, this is because if we do not know what *is*, we cannot say what *should be*. The previous chapters have offered an explanation of the former. The core conclusion is that currency markets are dominated by short-term capital flows, which are in turn driven largely by psychology as guided by agents' mental model. As a consequence, the international economy may be marked by, among other things, large, chronic trade imbalances, exchange-rate volatility, and bandwagon effects. The imbalances occur because one price cannot, except by coincidence, clear two markets at once; the latter two are not only problems in and of themselves, but they contribute to currency crises which, particularly in developing nations, may cause considerable harm to a macroeconomy. Exchange rates do not automatically adjust to make our lives more pleasant.

What should be done? In general, Post Keynesians pursue policies that generate high levels of output and employment. Price and financial market stability are also desirable, largely because they are assumed to contribute to the ends previously mentioned. The international monetary system as currently designed frustrates these goals in a number of ways:

1   Currency prices are mis-determined because they are driven by short-term time horizons instead of long.[1]
2   Currency price volatility reduces the expectation of profit from investment and, therefore, the level of aggregate demand.
3   Currency price mis-determination and volatility reduce the level of world trade.
4   Currency markets contribute to developing countries' woes.
5   The manner in which the international monetary system operates tends to create contraction and unemployment.

Each of these will be addressed in turn, after which measures that can avoid them will be outlined. Note that there will be overlap among these descriptions, particularly since all are related in one way or another to financial capital markets.

CURRENCY MARKET PROBLEMS

Throughout all that follows, it is important to remember how closely currency and asset markets are related in the real world. As explained in Chapter Three, nothing is more important in foreign exchange rate determination than the flow of portfolio capital. When agents expect a currency to appreciate, they buy assets denominated in that currency; and when a particular country's assets become more popular, so the money in which they are denominated will appreciate.

Inappropriate time horizons and mis-determined exchange rates

In Chapter Twelve of the *General Theory*, Keynes starts by examining the decision to undertake physical investment and then shifts almost imperceptibly into a discussion of the stock market. He does so on the assumption that, "… the daily revaluations of the Stock Exchange, though they are primarily made to facilitate transfers of old investments between one individual and another, *inevitably exert a decisive influence on the rate of current investment*" (emphasis added; Keynes 1964: 151). This is so, he says, because, "… there is no sense in building up a new enterprise at a cost greater than that at which a similar existing enterprise can be purchased" (Keynes 1964: 151). If the stock prices of firms that make furniture are declining, those considering building or expanding such a company will take this as a negative sign. Thus, stock market valuations directly impact on the expected rate of profit from investment variable (π^e).[2] This is shown in equation 5.5:

$$I = (r_{us}, \pi^e) \qquad\qquad 5.5$$
$$\;\; - \quad +$$

One of Keynes' central concerns in this regard was that the influence of asset markets on physical investment would tend to shift the time horizon used to make such decisions. Physical investment is a long-term phenomenon. The consequences of building a factory, restaurant, retail shop, for example, extend well into the future, beyond, in fact, the range over which one might have a chance of generating a reasonable forecast. Still, a forecast must be made if a decision is to be rendered. In doing so, a number of weighty factors must be considered, among them being one's managerial and marketing skills, consumer tastes, technology, competition, government regulations, and so on. The investor must study not only the current states of these variables, but possible future ones, as well as those affecting all potential competitors. These deliberations are terribly important because once the physical investment process is underway, there is no realistic means of reversing it. Changing your mind once underway will almost certainly mean lost money, perhaps substantial amounts thereof. You cannot decide overnight to no longer be a restaurateur without incurring significant costs, so it is illogical to constantly reevaluate the profitability of your restaurant when the physical capital invested cannot be magically changed into a shoe shop. Consequently, agents can be expected to take this very seriously and they will expend a considerable amount of effort at the forecasting stage. In terms of economic outcomes, this is as it should be. The investment decision, for the individual and the community, will be better done if agents spend time and effort considering it.

In the stock market, however, one can divest oneself of an asset in moments. There is little need to undertake the burdensome task of doing the careful research mentioned above because the average cost of an error is so much lower. In such circumstances, market participants find that their energies are more profitably spent forecasting the psychology of the market – what Keynes called "speculation" (Keynes 1964: 158). The rest of the market, too, will likely have a very short time horizon since agents have no strong connection to the asset in question. Thus, speculative forecasts rarely look very far into the future.

This has an inevitable effect on new physical investment. The short-run mentality creates (in combination with the heuristics mentioned in Chapter Three) a tendency to overreact to information. Just because, for example, there has been a rise in the price of raw chicken should not necessarily mean that there will be a large impact on the long-run profitability of a restaurant chain that specializes in poultry dishes. Everything else being equal, they may well be able to make adjustments (including shifting to another specialty) which allow them to keep profits at or near current levels. They frankly do not have a choice – as mentioned above, they cannot suddenly change their restaurant into a shoe store. Since they cannot now choose whether or not they run a restaurant, they accept the new market conditions and start working on a solution. But those dealing in secondary sales of the company's stock may well take the rise in costs as a sign to begin an exit. Their primary concern is what other asset-market participants will think, not how the management team will adapt. In fact, the low cost of divesting themselves of assets means that they and their colleagues probably knew relatively little about the restaurant business in the first place. Thus, their ignorance will contribute to their decision. "Surely," they will think, "a rise in the cost of raw chicken is a bad thing – sell!"

This may have direct effects on the company itself. First of all, the stockholders are the true owners of the firm. If the falling stock price is seen as an indication of bad management, then managers may be replaced. Alternatively, there could be a buy-out of the enterprise in question. Financial institutions may perceive the falling stock price as a negative, making loans more expensive and thus frustrating management attempts to address the underlying issue. In any event, the firm's managers may be forced into plans of action that raise the short-run stock price rather than solve the long-run problem. These two courses may not always be incompatible, but when they are the incentive will be to select the former. In summary, the short-run orientation of financial investment is imparted to physical capital formation, with the consequence being that those conducting the latter may find themselves in a situation where they must spend more time and effort satisfying stock owners than truly solving problems.

Returning to currency markets, the fact that they are so closely tied to financial capital means that forecasts there, too, have an unreasonably short time horizon and are hence "mis-determined." National currencies should logically reflect the relative value of the goods and services produced in that country (as related to the current account) and the profitability of firms based there (as related to the capital account). These are the ultimate reasons for holding the money issued by a particular state and if markets were driven only by these then we would witness currency-market participants thinking long and hard about committing to a particular foreign currency and changing their minds only when considerable evidence had accumulated to convince them that their earlier, well-considered opinions were wrong. But, instead, it is Keynes' game of musical chairs on a global scale. This cannot be proved directly, but look back at the figures in Chapter Six showing the movement of the dollar since the collapse of Bretton Woods. Is it really possible to justify the massive swings we have witnessed in terms of some set of fundamental factors related to relative appeal of US goods and services or the profitability of US enterprises? Even Neoclassical economists doubt this; Post Keynesians simply reject it.

None of this would be terribly relevant if currency prices had little connection to real economic activity. But exchange rates are terribly important signals in the allocation of physical and financial resources. It has been argued even by those in the Neoclassical camp that currency price speculation can have consequences that are "devastating for particular sectors and whole economies" (Eichengreen, Tobin, and Wyplosz 1995: 164). This is particularly so for small, developing economies where the underlying base is fragile at best. As described at the end of Chapter Six, currency crises, caused in part by these short-term biases, can lead to social disasters for those least equipped to deal with them. Even the day in, day out movement of currency prices in a system like ours is suspect. Mis-determined exchange rates lead to a misallocation of resources because they are not sending the appropriate signals to those involved in the activities that create output and employment. Government policy makers, too, often find themselves implementing policies that are designed to please the portfolio investors who are driving the currency market rather than solving economic problems.

Currency price volatility and the expectation of profit from investment

Not only does the undue influence of asset markets mean that currency prices are mis-determined, but that they are also volatile. As explained in Chapter Three, volatility is a direct function of uncertainty, availability, representativeness, anchoring, the desire for quick results, animal spirits, and convention. Their effect is greatly magnified by the short time-horizon of portfolio investment. Hence, forecasts are subject to frequent revision, and along with them the portfolios of agents (which then drives currency prices).

What this means for output and employment is that rapidly fluctuating currency prices add to the environment of uncertainty within which entrepreneurs must already operate. Such an effect might not only increase liquidity preference and thus reduce spending and raise the cost of cash, but it may also directly reduce the expected rate of profit from investment. As Keynes argues in Chapter Twelve of the *General Theory*, in the absence of our innate tendency to action rather than inaction, very little physical investment would take place (Keynes 1964: 161). A volatile currency market simply adds one more, unfortunately rather prominent, variable to the list of those with the potential to upset "the delicate balance of spontaneous optimism" (Keynes 1964: 162).

Currency price volatility, mis-determination, and world trade

It is easy to imagine that the conditions described above would be particularly discouraging to entrepreneurs in the import/export sector. For them, a rapidly changing currency price is not just a symbol of uncertainty, it is a direct and significant influence on their profits. Beyond the short-term volatility, the sort of long swings we have witnessed in currency prices since the fall of Bretton Woods would also have a deep impact on firms' viability. Smaller firms would be the hardest hit, leaving us with a less competitive world economy, which has negative repercussions for income distribution and aggregate demand.

Currency markets and the developing world

Everything said above applies to both the developed and developing world; however, the consequences for the latter tend to be more serious. Keynes' "delicate balance of spontaneous optimism" is especially tenuous in the developing world and even the milder volatility and price swings we see in developed economies would be sufficient to destabilize them; instead, they tend to be much greater. Furthermore, the very threat of events like those that occurred in Mexico and Thailand may be sufficient to discourage those wishing to undertake economic activity. At the very least, the sort of investment that takes place will be affected, with the likely result that real will suffer relative to financial (and the Mexican and Thai data in Chapter Six indicated). The myriad other problems faced by developing states who decide to open their stock markets to international investors has been amply covered by Ilene Grabel and will not be discussed here (see, for example, Grabel 1999). Suffice it to say that the current structure of the international monetary system tends not to encourage economic development and the default "solution" of liberalizing portfolio capital markets has not only served to make matters worse, it has meant that other programs have not been pursued instead.

Currency prices, trade flows, and contractionary tendencies

The last problem created by the current structure of the international monetary system is again related to the dominant role of financial capital, but not as directly. Recall from Chapter Four that a flexible exchange rate system can be in equilibrium even if there are trade imbalances. This is in contrast to Neoclassicism's view which argues that, at least over the long run, exchange rates act as an equilibrating mechanism for less-competitive countries and thereby create balanced trade. Hence, nations faced with a potential drain on economic activity – i.e., a trade deficit – can rest assured that currency prices will soon move to correct this problem. For them, foreign exchange rates thus play a role analogous to interest rates in keeping injections and leakages at the level that guarantees full employment.

Their view is premised on the idea that capital flows are very small and arise primarily as a means of financing trade imbalances. In reality, however, the overwhelming majority of currency transactions are related to autonomous short-term capital flows. Even when large trade deficits create significant problems for a macroeconomy, it is more common that they be offered new financing options than be forced to reduce imports to the level of exports (Shaikh 1980 and 1996 and Shaikh and Antonopoulos 1998). In short, our exchange rate system does not operate so as to automatically correct trade imbalances (the subject of Chapter Four); that this is true is due to the role played by capital flows.

This is not a new theme in Post Keynesian exchange rate literature. Keynes (1980) argued this, and Davidson has continued to do so: "Keynes … recognized that large, unfettered capital flows could create serious international payments problems for nations whose current accounts could otherwise be roughly in balance" (Davidson 2002: 481). Though it is likely that, as balance-of-payments-growth constraint theorists have argued, non-price variables play a significant role in driving trade flows so that exchange rate movements might not be sufficient to completely eliminate imbalances. It would nevertheless be preferable to observe that the currencies of trade deficit nations depreciated while those of surplus countries appreciated.

The above is not so much an explanation of how exchange rates create a problem as how they do not automatically solve one. There is a systemic issue, however, and it is as follows. While it is true that nations with trade deficits can carry them indefinitely, ceteris paribus, they would rather not. It is a drain on employment and financial resources. And since currency prices, for the variety of reasons mentioned above, have no built-in tendency to correct the problem, often the only option available to concerned policy makers is a reduction in the overall level of domestic economic activity. This is an effective means of addressing the issue (consider the effect of a fall in Py given a relatively flat BTFX in the open-economy Z-D diagram), but one that causes a contraction in the level of economic activity both at home and abroad. The likelihood of this scenario emerging is much greater when the organization of an international payments system, in spite of the fact that it is much less painful for those with a surplus to spend more than those with a deficit to spend less, places the burden of adjustment on the deficit country (Davidson 1992–93 and 1999). And, as shown in Chapter Four, the larger the autonomous capital flows, the larger can trade imbalances become. Thus, the operation of our exchange rate system introduces to policy a contractionary bias, as those with trade deficits may have an incentive to shrink their economies. As their imports fall, so the deflation is passed on to their trading partners, who may respond in kind.

POLICY

The current structure of the international monetary system causes currency prices to be mis-determined and volatile, reducing the expectation of profit from investment and the volume of world trade. This contributes to developing countries' problems and imparts a contractionary bias to economies throughout the world. Solving this requires, first and foremost, a significant reduction in the volume of international financial capital flows. Surely the evidence of the past thirty-plus years is sufficient to bury the orthodox view of liquidity once and for all. It is high time to admit that it is simply not true that allowing free flows of portfolio capital, alone, somehow encourages economic growth and development. Instead, what we get is distortion and volatility. To quote Keynes only slightly out of context, the conditions necessary for the Neoclassical story to be true "happen not to be those of the economic society in which we actually live, with the result that its teaching is misleading and disastrous if we attempt to apply it to the facts of experience" (Keynes 1964: 3).

The limitation of portfolio capital flows can be accomplished in a variety of ways, as outlined below. That is the central recommendation of this volume. In addition, Paul Davidson's suggestions with respect to reform of the international monetary system are relevant here and will be reviewed. Last, a few words are said on the issue of fixed versus flexible exchange rates.

Capital controls

The core of any successful international monetary reform lies in the implementation of capital controls. *The ultimate goal of these would be to eliminate mis-determination and volatility by forcing market participants to take more care in the research undertaken prior to the physical or financial investment decision and to feel a stronger bond to the asset once purchased.* Note that setting out to change those interested in quick profits into long-term investors is not likely to be a realistic ambition. Rather, we simply want to discourage those in the former group as much as possible, without adversely affecting the participation of those in the latter.[3]

A tax on exchange rate transactions is often proposed as a remedy. The fact that one of the proponents for this idea (sometimes called a "Tobin Tax") comes from the Neoclassical camp is an indicator of the severity of the problem discussed here (Tobin 1978). The basic idea is that a levy in the range of 0.1 to 1 percent be placed on all exchange rate transactions, thus discouraging those made only in pursuit of capital gain while, at the same time, generating funds for use in economic development. Unfortunately, such a small cost is very unlikely to have an impact when typical exchange rate swings are more than sufficient to generate speculative profits (or the hope thereof) well in excess of that amount (Davidson 1997). Furthermore, taxes high enough to have a substantial effect on portfolio capital flows would probably serve as an even greater deterrent to long-term investment. This is not to say that a Tobin tax or something similar might not play some useful role, but by itself it would be rather feeble and would not be applied with the selectivity necessary to achieve the main goal.

What would be preferable is something similar to the program Chile employed from 1991 to 1998 (Neeley 1999: 25). Although its characteristics changed over time, the central features were a requirement to keep funds in Chile for a prescribed period, a compensating mandatory deposit with the central bank (non-interest paying), and a penalty for early withdrawal. Each of these was more stringent for portfolio capital flows than direct and thus properly discriminated between the two sets of investors. Whether these were effective or not depends on who you read. Ilene Grabel, a Post Keynesian, is a supporter and argues that such a system could effectively prevent the outbreak of a financial crisis, mitigate the effects if one occurred, and limit contagion (Grabel 2003 – this is an outstanding article that I highly recommend). While the reactions of Neoclassical authors are mixed, some actually align themselves with Grabel and there appears to be agreement even among detractors that the composition of capital flows shifted away from the short and toward the long term (Neeley 1999). This is precisely the goal. It is instructive to observe that Chile suffered no fallout from the Mexican crisis in 1994 or the Asian in 1997. The measures have now been dismantled, however, leading Grabel to comment:

> In my view, the decision to terminate inflow management was imprudent given the substantial risks of unregulated short-term inflows and the risk that Chile could be destabilised by emergent crises in Argentina and Brazil. It would have been far more desirable to maintain the controls at a low level, while addressing the current account deficit and the need to attract inflows through other means. Indeed, flexible deployment of the inflows policy was a hallmark of the Chilean model (consistent with trip wires – speed bumps), and it is regrettable that authorities abandoned this course.
>
> (Grabel 2003: 327)

I strongly agree both in terms of the need to control the short-term flows and in the necessity of governments maintaining flexibility in this regard. It is all but certain that not only will market conditions change, but investors will seek ways around regulations. Thus, we cannot expect to simply put policy in place and sit back. Ensuring that all clearing must take place through the central bank would be helpful in this regard. This would greatly enhance the power that each nation would have "to monitor and, if desired, to control movements of flight capital" (Davidson 1992–93: 158).

The strength and precise nature of the regulations implemented is a question that can only be answered on a case-by-case basis. In general, developing states will require greater efforts to limit financial capital flows, along with closer supervision and larger imposed costs. This is not to say that developed-country asset markets cannot create significant distortions and other problems, but when they do occur it is against a more stable backdrop than in the developing world. Whatever exact limitations on financial capital flows are put into place, the policy makers involved must also create a system of trip wires and speed bumps to guide them (see Grabel 2003 for an extended description). The former give advanced warning of trouble. Assuming that business and government enterprises can be trusted to make transparent the important numbers in question, economists can monitor them for indicators of crisis like those mentioned at the end of Chapter Five and in the discussions of the Mexican and Asian incidents in Chapter Six. These would include debt-to-income ratios, relative levels of foreign debt, relative levels of short-term debt, and official foreign exchange reserves (all mentioned in the Chapter Five discussion of crisis). The signals generated do not guarantee that a problem is about to occur, but they serve as a heads-up to policy makers that action may need to be taken. They should also act as a guide to longer-term policy adjustments. If, for example, it is found that domestic agents are taking on increasing levels of foreign debt, then regulations should be revised accordingly. A caveat here is that one must exercise care in reducing barriers to short-term capital on the assumption that low realized levels of the latter indicate that it is no longer an issue – it may simply be that the regulations are doing their job and removing them may cause a resurgence!

With respect to speed bumps, these slow the rate of capital flows and thereby attempt to defuse a budding crisis. Grabel explains,

> Speed bumps can take many forms. Examples include measures that require borrowers to unwind positions involving locational or maturity mismatches, curb the pace of imports or foreign borrowing, limit the fluctuation or convertibility of the currency, or slow the exit and particularly the entry of portfolio investment. I emphasise the importance of speed bumps governing inflows rather than outflows because measures that merely target outflows are more apt to trigger and exacerbate panic than to prevent it.
>
> (Grabel 2003: 323).

These may give policy makers time to formulate plans and might let cooler heads prevail in the market.

One of the nice things about capital controls, trip wires, and speed bumps is that they may be employed unilaterally to great effect. It is not necessary for all nations to employ the same or even similar systems, though there would definitely be advantages to such an eventuality (particularly in terms of a general shift in the structure of world capital flows). But, as has been shown in Chile, Colombia, Malaysia, South Korea, the United States, and so on, it is entirely possible for a single nation to find success putting into place rules that apply only within its borders (notwithstanding potential formal and informal sanctions from other Neoclassically oriented nations and international "relief" organizations around the world). The goal of reducing the effect of exchange rate volatility and mis-determination can largely be solved one country at a time and the positive results can then be used to break down resistance elsewhere.

Burden of adjustment placed on surplus countries

The implementation of capital controls throughout the world would help to bring on what might be called the euthanasia of the speculator and get us most of the way to a monetary system that created a stable environment which supported output and employment growth. It would greatly reduce volatility and mis-determination, thereby increasing the expected rate of profit from investment and world trade. In addition, if portfolio capital flows were a smaller portion of total currency demand, we should expect to see smaller and shorter-lived trade imbalances. This would reduce the significance of the balance-of-payments growth constraint, make nations less likely to engage in deflationary policies to reduce imports, and lead to smoothly adjusting and more predictable exchange rates that should encourage agents to engage in output and employment creating activities across national borders.

Paul Davidson's writings have generally supported the above ideas, while adding extra measures. He has proposed an international monetary system based on an International Money Clearing Unit, or IMCU (Davidson 1992–93, 1997, 1999, 2002, and 2003; Davidson credits Keynes with many of the central features). The IMCU would be held only by central banks, and would be used to settle accounts and act as the reserve asset. Each country would set an initial exchange rate of domestic currency units per IMCU, which would be fixed until the parties in question decide to change it. Unlike Bretton Woods, where it was incumbent on the deficit country to ask to have their currency devalued (which was politically unpalatable and something the surplus countries fought), here the burden is shifted to the surplus nation. Therein lies the key to the system and the solution to the problem of the bias toward contractionary policies. Once a surplus reaches a certain, prearranged level, the surplus country must either spend it (on imports or direct foreign investment into any other member of the clearing union, or as unilateral transfers to deficit members) or it will be confiscated and redistributed to debtor members. One way or another, this means that the funds accumulated by nations on the right of BTFX on the Post Keynesian open economy Z-D diagram (Figure 5.7) re-enter via upward D shifts for other members of the clearing union (in stark contrast to the downward D shifts in systems where the burden is on the deficit country). Only if a deficit country is rich and already at full employment are they forced to bear the burden of adjustment (via devaluation). Otherwise, the goal is to continue to inject money into the income stream and thereby keep the world economy expanding.[4]

The mechanism by which exchange rates would be adjusted is by relating them to efficiency wages, or the nominal wage divided by the average product of labor. As efficiency wages rise (due either to a rise in nominal wages or a fall in productivity), so a currency would lose value relative to the IMCU, and vice versa.[5] This not only creates another mechanism whereby trade balances will tend toward zero (assuming labor productivity and wages to be the central factors in determining the international competitiveness of goods and services), but it insulates each nation from the others' inflation (Davidson 1992–93: 162–3).

Such a system, in combination with the goal of limiting portfolio capital flows, would create incentives to keep levels of economic activity high, channel funds to the most destitute, and allow individual nations to pursue more or less independent economic policies. Two mechanisms would operate to reduce imbalances: the linking of currency values to efficiency wages and the trigger mechanism whereby surplus nations are forced to spend. Exchange rates are more stable and no longer mis-determined, the limitation on capital flows eliminates the role of bandwagon effects, and the system no longer contains a deflationary bias. Hopefully, given such a fertile ground for growth, nations would also choose to pursue policies that achieve full employment – something with benefits that would multiply and spread to all the trading partners.

Fixed versus flexible exchange rates

The typical orthodox textbook discussion of exchange rate policy centers on whether we should have fixed or flexible rates. Generally speaking, the conclusion is that, despite the fact that within countries we use fixed systems within their borders, we should favor the latter. This is premised on the idea that flexible rates yield balanced trade and other efficiencies.

Though Davidson's system has fixed rates as one of its features, whether or not we let currencies float is, in some respects, a secondary issue. While it is true that stable rates would avoid the problems associated with volatility, it is not necessarily true that having a fixed rate yields stability. In the absence of measures to limit portfolio capital, speculative attacks may force governments to continue to move pegs into ranges they can defend, thus creating the very volatility they had hoped to avoid. Davidson is well aware of this, of course, and his recommendations do include capital controls to make the fixed rates more manageable. Without that, his system (as he realizes) is untenable.

CONCLUSIONS

The current structure of the currency market is such that it allows short-term capital flows to dominate exchange rate determination. This, in turn, means that we experience chronic trade imbalances, misallocation of resources, depressed levels of economic activity, a contractionary bias to the international monetary system, and occasional catastrophic crises. What is recommended here is not a rejection of markets, but a modification. It is in that sense not a radical set of policies that is being advocated, and yet one would think so given the reactions of most economists and policy makers to the suggestion of capital controls. Particularly since the fall of communism and the rise of globalization, there seems to be an increasing willingness to trust in the logic of market solutions, particularly and ironically where they are most suspect: financial capital. While there are occasional waves of sentiment for reforms such as those recommended here (in the wake of the Asian crises or the US sub-prime loan debacle, for example), it appears that those in power and those who advise and elect them suffer from the same short memories as Minsky's representative agents.

8   Conclusions

At the time of this writing, the world economy is full of uncertainty. The dollar continues its historic collapse, US financial markets are in post-subprime crisis mode, oil prices are rising and threatening to trigger inflation and contraction, incomes are becoming increasingly uneven, religious and ethnic conflicts continue unabated and spread their effects far beyond the borders of the nations in question, global warming endangers our environment, and catastrophic natural disasters add to the challenges we already face. On the other hand, the incredible acceleration in the rate of technological and productivity growth that started with the Industrial Revolution continues. Our technical ability to address problems is unparalleled in human history and there simply is no longer any reason for people anywhere in the world to be hungry, cold, or scared. The only real obstacles that we face are philosophical; unfortunately, they are formidable.

This was equally true during the Great Depression. In the United States, for example, it was the very ease with which goods and services and particularly physical capital could be produced that caused the problem by saturating demand and leaving us with the bitter irony of excess capacity in the face of desperate want. The difficulty was not in devising a means by which to effectively boost economic activity, but to develop a policy that was perceived as right and just and fair. The New Deal was resisted not because people did not think it would work, but because it was viewed (particularly by those in the business community) as "socialist" and therefore un-American.

What ended the debate was the Japanese attack on Pearl Harbor. Not only did US mobilization for war accomplish the New Deal's goals on a far grander scale, but the American public, and even business interests, had absolutely no difficulty reconciling the consequent massive intrusion of the state into private affairs with the ideals of life, liberty, and the pursuit of happiness. The American economy exploded and unemployment dropped to nothing. The means to accomplish this had existed back in 1929, only the will was missing.

Today, too, it is a lack of will that prevents us from putting into place the policies that encourage economic growth and prosperity. Blind faith in the writings of 18th century political economists has created a roadblock far more formidable than any technological one. People applaud markets as if they were perfect, infallible, and, indeed, sacred, brought down from Mount Sinai by Moses along with the other commandments. The truth is, of course, that they are only tools, one of many means by which we may try to solve social problems. As such, they can be quite useful and they are so in many instances – but not every instance and often not without significant modification. It has been demonstrated in this book, for example, that allowing free reign to market forces in foreign exchange rate determination and international capital flows can create numerous problems, especially in the developing world. It is high time to be pragmatic and not dogmatic.

Nor are half measures in order. As Paul Davidson writes,

> The problems facing the international payments system are not easily resolved. If we start with the defeatist attitude that it is too difficult to change the awkward system in which we are enmeshed, then no progress will be made. We must reject such defeatism at this exploratory stage and merely ask whether these particular proposals for improving the operations of the international payments system to promote global growth will create more difficulties than other proposed innovations. The health of the world economic system will not permit us to muddle through!
>
> (Davidson 1992–93: 178)

Unfortunately, those of us in the Post Keynesian and Institutionalist camps find ourselves largely shut out of not only policy circles but also excluded from the training of new economists. Thus, meeting Davidson's challenge may be very difficult.

I believe that the two most fruitful paths for us to follow in getting our voices heard may be through the work of policy institutes and in the classroom. Ideally, we should try to influence policy by first changing the theory. However, that strategy is probably the least promising, given the state of our discipline today. It is very unlikely, for a number of reasons, that we could even gain an audience with those whose opinions shape contemporary mainstream economics. And, even if we could, changing the minds of those who have already self selected into that paradigm seems doubtful. On the other hand, why should we even select that route when our relative strength is empirical, institutional, and historical studies of real-world phenomena, something that would be unlikely to earn a Neoclassical economist tenure, let alone convince them of their errors in a debate over theory?

Instead, I propose that we highlight and expand our efforts in policy analysis and country and area studies. If we are correct about the way economic systems really work, it will show up here much more distinctly than it would in a set of theoretical equations or graphs. Groups like the Center for Full Employment and Price Stability, the Economic Policy Institute, the Levy Institute, the Schwartz Center for Economic Policy Analysis, and the University of Texas Inequality Project are already doing excellent work in this area. The meltdown of the US financial system came as no surprise to anyone in any of these organizations, and successes like that should be advertised far and wide so that economists and non-economists alike know who is getting it right and who is getting it wrong. In addition, I would be very keen to see one of the existing institutes or a new one undertake the mission of monitoring the trip wires mentioned in Chapter Seven. Were we to publish regular data on the financial conditions in developing nations this would not only create and disseminate terribly important information, but it might actually have some impact on policy.

It is also desperately important for us to continue to develop models that reflect our core concepts *and to teach them to our students*. As everyone who reads this book knows, there is no one more open to Post Keynesianism and Institutionalism than the undergraduate. As neophytes, they come to us with the assumption that economics is a discipline that focuses on real-world issues like business cycles, trade relations, and mark-up pricing. Instead, they find themselves learning about rational expectations, autarky, and helicopter-assisted money supply growth. It is essential that they are introduced to our alternative before they are completely turned off by our field of study or stop asking probing questions and are assimilated. If we do this, then at the very worst the end product will be a more broadly educated economist who at least understands that other options exist, even if they do not accept them; but if experience is any guide, we are more likely to end up with much more than that. Accomplishing this requires that instructors do not postpone telling students about Keynes and Veblen until the end of the semester, once all the Neoclassical material has been covered. Nor should they, heaven forbid, make their sole effort the recommendation of outside reading. Make it the core of the course. We must teach Post Keynesianism and Institutionalism at the undergraduate level. If we do so, not only will our students emerge with a much better understanding of the manner in which economies really operate, but we will generate new demand for our doctoral programs, demand from young men and women who are actually interested in learning *economics* and not simply finding a discipline in which they can practice their math skills.

Notes

1 Introduction

1 Domanick Salvatore's states, for example: "... empirical results do not provide much support for these theories ..." (Salvatore 2004: 530).
2 One might interject here, "But surely trade must return to balance eventually?" This is no more likely in the Post Keynesian framework than is full employment, which is not to say that it cannot happen, but that there is no overriding tendency towards that state. There may be some forces pushing us in that direction, but these are neither alone nor dominant. This will be further developed in chapters three through five.
3 Note that this does not rule out the possibility of non-conformism. Indeed, if behavior patterns reproduced themselves perfectly then there would never be evolution (non-conformism being one of many sources of change).
4 Something that is just as true (albeit for different reasons) in mainstream economics, though this is often forgotten.
5 For present purposes, it makes no difference whether these values are nominal or real.
6 Note that mainstream economists do not truly believe that agents know the future. Instead, it is their belief that so assuming makes the structure of the underlying argument simpler without changing the basic result. Post Keynesians disagree strongly with the latter.
7 Note that there are many more sophisticated Neoclassical models than this. However, it is the contention of Post Keynesian economists that they all reduce essentially to this: in the absence of frictions or outside interference, the economy tends to full employment and money and other financial variables are long-run neutral.
8 One final note: though the approach developed is mean to be a general one, my research has focused almost exclusively on currency price movements among developed countries (particularly the United States, Germany, and Japan). The analysis in this text may therefore be biased in that direction.

2 Neoclassical approaches to exchange rate determination

1 For those seeking a useful Neoclassically oriented textbook on exchange rates, I highly recommend Laurence Copeland's (2005). It is by far my favorite. The graphical analyses of the monetary and Dornbusch models in this chapter are adapted from that he uses in his text. Hans Visser's (2006) is another very good one.
2 Note that the assumption that markets are natural adds support to the argument that institutional and historical analysis is of limited usefulness as compared to basing premises on reasoning.
3 Other commonly mentioned characteristics of Neoclassical economics are an emphasis on marginal analysis and on the individual decision maker.

4 For another version of the full-employment assumption, see the explanation of the process by which I=S in chapter one.

5 I would suspect that at least some Neoclassical economists would deny the assumption of full employment in their analysis. If that is the case then it is very difficult to understand why no explanation of currency prices has been offered that allows portfolio capital a role in determining currency prices.

6 For convenience, the rest of the text is written as if there are two "countries" in the world: the United States and the rest of the world.

7 To give another example, in 1998, average daily turnover in foreign currency markets was $372 trillion (based on the Bank for International Settlement's currency market survey of that year: Bank for International Settlements 1999). During that same year, world exports were $5.5 trillion (International Monetary Fund 2002) and world direct foreign investment inflows were $694 billion (UNCTAD 2002). Assuming that for every customer transaction, banks find it necessary to undertake further covering operations, each dollar of trade and direct foreign investment must generate a few dollars more in currency market activity; let us say that four hedge transactions of the same size are undertaken per customer-generated deal. This means that each dollar of trade and direct foreign investment must be multiplied by five to give a real sense of their share of the total foreign exchange market (data from the Federal Reserve Bank of New York suggests that the number might really be closer to three (Cross 1998: 15); I selected five so as to bias the argument against the case I am trying to make). Doing so for 1998 yields $31 trillion for their combined value. As the total for the market was $372, this leaves $341. Subtracting from that 10 percent of the total to take account of possible official intervention leaves $303.8 trillion to represent portfolio foreign investment (if data collected by Rasmus Fatum are accurate, 10 percent is a gross overestimate (Fatum 2000); again, the goal is to bias the argument against the conclusion that portfolio capital flows dominate the currency market). Assuming the same ratio of covering transactions by banks, means that $60.8 trillion in gross portfolio foreign investment took place in 1998. This is over *ten times* the size of world trade that year.

8 An additional curiosity regarding purchasing power parity is the fact that, though it is in essence a theory of trade flows, there is no income variable. This is, in one sense, consistent with the assumption of full employment. If income remains constant or grows at a similarly constant (natural) rate across countries, then it will not show up as a determinant of changes in trade flows. Only prices would be important.

9 Authors actually cite the natural rate of growth, rather than full employment in particular.

10 Interest rates can be incorporated into the model by allowing them to change V (or, technically, V's inverse, the ratio of desired nominal money balances to nominal income). Specifically, as interest rates rise, so V increases and y^d shifts up. The underlying logic is that as interest rates rise, so the demand for cash falls (and that for bonds rises). If there has been no change in the money supply, the fall in money demand creates an excess supply of cash, which agents will spend. The resulting shifts appear exactly as those shown in Figure 2.2.

11 The greatest success has been found in studying countries with extremely high inflation and over very long time horizons (Shaikh and Antonopoulos: 1998).

12 Though actually an antecedent to the monetary model, it is more convenient to save interest rate parity until immediately before the Dornbusch model, in which it will be used.

13 Note that the time horizon of the expectations and the term of each interest rate must be the same.

14 As above, the time horizon of the forward exchange rate and the term of each interest rate must be the same.

15 Note that this means that the interest rate will not play the role it did in the monetary model. This is a considerable improvement.

16 Note that this implies that currency market participants routinely operate with forecasts with time horizons of three to five years.

17 The mechanism by which it is argued that prices adjust has undergone numerous changes over the years. The one certain thing one can say is that they do eventually rise!

18 All the while there is no further adjustment in $(\$/FX)^e$. It reacts only when something affecting the long-term equilibrium changes. That something must, of course, be related to the monetary model.

19 Bear in mind that when Q=1, purchasing power parity holds. If Q>1, then we must lie on a point to the right of the PPP curve (domestic trade surplus) and when Q<1 we must be to the left (domestic trade deficit).

20 This last addition has always struck me as somewhat inconsistent. The y^d curve is derived from MV=Py. There is no exchange rate in that equation, and yet we have suddenly added one. Indeed, the model will not work without that addition. One could argue that it represents the fact that different nominal exchange rates trigger inflows and outflows of capital, which then affect the domestic money supply. This is not entirely satisfactory either, however, as in an economy experiencing a temporary trade surplus (for example) it is never shown how the capital inflows exit the economy and leave it affected only by the initial change in nominal money supply.

21 Of course, it is really a set of simultaneous equations so that everything is happening at once – but it is easier to think in terms of a sequence of events.

22 Note that this approach still keeps historical/institutional detail to a minimum, employs an axiomatic mathematical framework, and maintains a free market bias (which is implied in the lesson that government policy tends to disturb the economy from its long-run natural growth path).

23 This is compounded by the modeler's decision that agents would employ the monetary model in their forecast. There is certainly no evidence of this in the real world. This is another reminder of the fact that Neoclassical economics prefers deduction ("this seems like a reasonable assumption") to induction ("I should poll currency dealers and find out what particular model they use in making forecasts").

24 Of course, at that point it would become relevant to raise objections to many of the other assumptions being made.

25 Rogoff (2001) argues that this continues to be the state of affairs today.

26 Which in turn was a result of the fact that currency market speculation had grown, creating a market for the surveys.

27 See Harvey (1998–99) for examples of these two tests.

28 Generally speaking, δ is found to be a negative number and the likelihood that equation 2.13 does not represent a significant relationship is rejected.

29 That "fundamentals" was adopted was no doubt due to the term's connotation in financial circles.

30 I have always wondered whether scholars employing definition by example in their research would give full credit to student papers that described, for instance, a business firm as "something like Citibank, WalMart, or Microsoft!"

31 Our desires can serve as a filter on how we interpret the real world, however, and that appears to be just what has happened here.

3 Psychology and decision-making in the foreign exchange market

1 Sections of this chapter are based on Harvey 1998 and Harvey 2006b.

2 For a brilliant study of the psychology of the currency market, see Oberlechner 2004. His work is based on original empirical research and looks at both the individual and social psychology of dealers. Post Keynesians and Institutionalists would thoroughly enjoy this work. For those who would like a deeper look at the issues raised in this chapter, Oberlechner's book is the definitive source.

3 Brokering is also an important segment of this market.

4 Retailers may appear to be offering two-way reciprocity as they are usually willing to buy or sell; but, these transactions are based simply on a mark up of the price paid by the retailer to the wholesaler. The one-way characterization of their currency market activity is a function of the fact that when contacting wholesalers to obtain the currency necessary to conduct customer business or to liquidate accumulated inventories, retailers are offering only to buy *or* sell.

5 For simplicity, central banks are ignored here. Their role in the post-Bretton Woods international economy, though occasionally noteworthy, has been minor for the most part.

6 For simplicity I assume that it is the importer who bears the burden of exchanging money.

7 It also means that they have in place already the staff and equipment necessary to play a more speculative role should they desire. This would be an activity that fell under commercial activities and not wholesaling.

8 It is, of course, possible to imagine circumstances under which their initial forecast and hence opening price could affect customers plans as they view those prices as indicative of market conditions.

9 This approach is adapted from that used by Keynes in chapter seventeen of the *General Theory* (Keynes 1964).

10 Note that in this particular example, the financial side of the economy is essentially following the real side and had no net impact, just as in the Neoclassical formulation. Post Keynesians do not deny that this can happen, only that it is not the only or, in today's economy, most likely possibility.

11 In some ways, it would have been better to avoid the word "bias" altogether given the chance for confusion, but that is precisely the term used in the psychology literature.

12 These would, of course, be related to other possible futures like central bank actions or industry developments.

13 Takatoshi Ito (1990) found direct evidence of this in foreign currency markets.

14 One could add a sixth: Conventional Wisdom. By this, Keynes means that there exist strong incentives to follow the crowd as "it is better for reputation to fail conventionally than to succeed unconventionally" (Keynes 1964: 158). However, this is really the same effect as discussed above under claiming credit and avoiding blame.

15 A very recent discovery is that biological factors, too, may play a role in creating volatility (Coates and Herbert 2008). In particular, "Cortisol is likely, therefore, to ... exaggerate the market's downward movement" (Coates and Herbert 2008: 6170) and "Testosterone, on the other hand, is likely to ... exaggerate the market's upward movement" (Coates and Herbert 2008: 6170–1). Of course, these effects are already included in the psychological variables and are merely the physiological means by which they take place.

16 Currency and financial crises are explained in chapter five.

17 Although the problem with Leeson was lack of supervision. The proper rules were in place (Cornford 1996).

18 Because with foreign currency for every agent holding an appreciating currency there must be someone holding a depreciating one, it might appear at first glance that this attitude toward risk always tends to balance out. That is not the case since some of those "letting it ride" will be pleasantly surprised by the sudden (if temporary) reversal of the trend caused by cash in. They will be delighted to find buyers for the otherwise unpopular currency and take this as their opportunity to eliminate at least part of the unwanted position, thus contributing to the whipsaw.

4 Leakages, injections, exchange rates, and trade (im)balances

1 Technically, it may be somewhat more complicated than this as injections and leakages can also include taxes and government expenditures and, in general, it is only required that *total* injections equal *total* leakages (and not necessarily that set associated with each sector); but, the basic story is still the same.

2 For simplicity I omit government intervention.

3 Technically, the sentence should read, "Foreign currency is offered to *dollar holders* when *foreign currency holders* wish to obtain dollars." However, for simplicity it will be assumed that only Americans supply dollars (i.e., are dollar holders) and only foreigners supply foreign currency (are foreign currency holders).
4 More straightforward in the sense that we will always be thinking in terms of what the agents in question want to achieve (purchase foreign assets, foreign goods and services, etc.) rather than which currency they happened to be holding (which then determines what they supply).
5 It is probably more realistic to measure the imports and exports in volume, but this gets rather complicated given this framework and the conclusion is no different.

5 Post Keynesian exchange rate modeling

1 For those unfamiliar with this approach, please see Davidson and Smolensky (1964), Davidson (1994), and Victoria Chick (1983). The Z-D analysis that follows draws primarily from Chick.
2 Note that this is quite distinct from money illusion, which assumes that agents cannot tell the difference between real and nominal values. Under Keynes, they know the difference, but economic actors face a world in which prices, wages, loans, contracts, et cetera, are all defined in nominal terms.
3 See Chick (1983) page 66 for this proof. The mathematics are not necessary to follow the discussion that follows.
4 Recall from chapter one the explanation of the process by which equilibrium savings comes to rest at the same level as equilibrium investment in both the Neoclassical and Post Keynesian schools. In the former, interest rates adjust to maintain the same (full-employment) level of output; in the latter, it is economic activity that adjusts, creating the very real possibility of involuntary unemployment over all time horizons.
5 Trade tends to be much more income than price elastic. Consequently, it is a shame that the impacts of P and y cannot be separated on BTFX. This is still superior to the purchasing power parity curve on the Monetary and Dornbusch Models, however, as the latter exclude changes in real income as factors entirely and assume (at least in the long run) that trade must be balanced.
6 This quadrant will generate the AER of chapter four, while BTFX shows the BTER.
7 Assume for simplicity that the consequent capital inflows are sterilized, otherwise a slight downward shift in MM may be necessary (though not enough to change our general results).
8 This assumes that the rise in US interest rates was unanticipated by ($/FX)e. Otherwise, the movement up the vertical axis on FXM could be partially or wholly offset by a rightward shift in the function.
9 The trade deficit would not cause a corresponding rightward shift in FXM since this would confuse the line of causation. It was the leftward shift in FXM that caused the trade deficit.
10 It is possible that agents may decide to focus on the rising unemployment and trade deficit in their mental model and thus forecast a dollar depreciation. If so, this would lead to a shift in FXM as expectations adjust. However, the history of the post-Bretton Woods currency market suggests that agents will almost always choose to focus instead on interest rate differentials.
11 And the net capital flows implied by the position of the economy on the BTFX curve means that, if they are not sterilized, the rise in r_{us} is dampened.
12 In Harvey (1993a), a study of daily currency price movements, it was found that it took a roughly two weeks of accumulated daily data to cause agents to change their medium term expectations.
13 Processes are formally defined as those economic activities that (within the mental model) directly impact on foreign currency prices.

14 Throughout this section the selection of the particular elements for the mental model was based both on surveys (see for example Cheung and Chinn 2000) and empirical research. For examples of the latter please see Harvey (1993a, 1998–99, 2002a, and 2004 and Harvey and Quinn 1997).

15 For an extensive review of the Post Keynesian view of interest rate parity in the context of endogenous money see Lavoie (2000, 2001, and 2002–03). Another set of excellent papers on the Post Keynesian view of interest rate parity is that by John Smithin (1999 and 2002–03).

16 Note that, in order to keep the currency-crisis schematic as simple as possible, π^e is being asked to do rather a lot. Not only is it the expected rate of profits from investment, but it is implied in the discussion above that it is ultimately and critically tied to realized returns. Furthermore, in the discussion that follows, it will be used to proxy rising incomes on the assumption that as π^e rises, so will physical investment and, ultimately, national output and income. While a more sophisticated representation of the macroeconomy would better trace that process, the conclusion for present purposes would be no different and the cost in additional clutter would be high. As π^e plays the central role, I opted to build the story around it.

6 Real-world applications

1 Much of this chapter is distilled from the wonderfully detailed "Treasury and Federal Reserve Exchange Operations" report in the *Federal Reserve Bulletin* (Board of Governors of the Federal Reserve System, various years). Descriptions of dollar movements not otherwise cited are taken from here.

2 Recall that the availability heuristic argues that agents place undue emphasis on dramatic events such as this.

3 Although the currency in question in no longer the mark, attention still tended to be focused on Germany in forecasting euro movements.

4 For an excellent Minksyian analysis of the crisis in general, see Arestis and Glickman (2002).

5 Readers interested in more sophisticated statistical analyses can see Akiba (2004), Harvey (1993a, 1998–99, 2002a, and 2004 and Harvey and Quinn 1997), and Mussa (2002, 2004, and 2007–08).

7 Problems and policy

1 I purposely avoided the term "misaligned" because it is already used to refer to exchange rates that do not generate balanced trade.

2 The reverse is also true, but to a more limited extent.

3 Resolving issues in the developing world require, incidentally, much more than the sort of reforms discussed here. My goal is simply to point out those problems created by exchange rates and capital flows. Those related to the core issues associated with the orientation of economic activity, a job well-suited for Veblenian Institutionalism, are not addressed here.

4 Implicit here is the outright rejection of the assumption of continuous full employment that is present in most Neoclassical analyses. Were economies always at full employment then Davidson's (and Keynes') fears would be misplaced. It is his contention, however, that because full employment is not guaranteed, chronic surplus nations represent an antisocial drain on economic activity. If they wish to continue to participate in the clearing union then they cannot act in a parasitic manner.

5 Recalling the Post Keynesian open economy Z-D diagram (Figure 5.7), a fall in the efficiency wage would simultaneously shift Z to the right (as W falls or apn rises in equation 5.3) and BTFX to the left (as the nation becomes more competitive and

therefore requires a more expensive domestic currency for balanced trade). Though this would create contradictory pressures with respect to trade flows, let us assume that the impact on competitiveness outweighs that of the rising P_y and the nation is left with a trade surplus (after beginning at balance) – even after D shifts up due to the surplus. What Davidson proposes is that the fixed exchange rate then move to reflect the shift in BTFX (which was in turn caused by the change in efficiency wages). Note that this has the effect of keeping trade balanced, or close to it.

Bibliography

Akiba, H. (2004) "Expectations, Stability, and Exchange Rate Dynamics under the Post Keynesian Hypothesis," *Journal of Post Keynesian Economics*, 27(1): 125–39.

Arestis, P. and Glickman, M. (2002) "Financial Crisis in Southeast Asia: Dispelling Illusion the Minskyan Way," *Cambridge Journal of Economics*, 26(2): 237–60.

Arestis, P., McCombie, J., and Vickerman, R. (2007) *Growth And Economic Development: Essays in Honour of A. P. Thirlwall*, Aldershot, UK: Edward Elgar.

Arestis, P. and Milberg, W. (1993–4) "Degree of Monopoly, Pricing, and Flexible Exchange Rates," *Journal of Post Keynesian Economics*, 16(2): 167–88.

Bank for International Settlements. (1994) 66th *Annual Report*, Basle, Switzerland: BIS.

Bank for International Settlements. (1996) *64th Annual Report*, Basle, Switzerland: BIS.

Bank for International Settlements. (1999) Triennial Central Bank Survey: Foreign Exchange and Derivatives Market Activity, 1998, Basle, Switzerland: BIS.

Bank for International Settlements. (2001) "PRESS RELEASE: Central bank survey of foreign exchange and derivatives market activity in April 2001: preliminary global data," Basel, Switzerland: BIS, 9 October.

Bank for International Settlements. (2002) *Triennial Central Bank Survey: Foreign Exchange and Derivatives Market Activity in 2001*, Basle, Switzerland: BIS.

Bank for International Settlements. (2005) *Triennial Central Bank Survey: Foreign Exchange and Derivatives Market Activity in 2004*, Basle, Switzerland: BIS.

Bishop, P. and Dixon, D. (1992) *Foreign Exchange Handbook: Managing Risk and Opportunity in Global Currency Markets*, New York: McGraw-Hill.

Board of Governors of the Federal Reserve System *Federal Reserve Bulletin*, various issues.

Branson, W.H. (1974) "Stocks and Flows in International Monetary Analysis," in A. Ando, R. Herring, and R. Martson (eds), *International Aspects of Stabilization Policies*, Boston: Federal Reserve Bank of Boston: 27–50.

Branson, W.H. (1983) "Macroeconomic Determinants of Real Exchange Risk," in R.J. Herring (ed.), *Managing Foreign Exchange Risk*, Cambridge: Cambridge University Press: 33–74.

Branson, W.H. and Haltunnen, Y.H. (1979) "Asset Market Determination of Exchange Rates: Initial Empirical and Policy Results," in J.P. Martin and A. Smith (eds), *Trade and Payments Adjustments under Flexible Exchange Rates*, London: Macmillan.

Bryant, R.C. (1987) *International Financial Intermediation*, Washington, D.C.: The Brookings Institution.

Cassel, G. (1923) *Money and Foreign Exchange after 1914*, New York: Macmillan.

Chang, H. and Grabel, I. (2004) *Reclaiming Development: An Alternative Economic Policy Manual*, London: Zed Books, Ltd.

Cheung, Y. and Chinn, M.D. (2000) "Currency Traders and Exchange Rate Dynamics: A Survey of the U.S. Market," University of California Santa Cruz Department of Economics Working Paper. Available online at: <http://econ.ucsc.edu/faculty/cheung/nysurvey.pdf> (accessed February 28, 2004).

Chick, V. (1983) *Macroeconomics After Keynes: A Reconsideration of the General Theory*, Cambridge, Massachusetts: MIT Press.

Chinn, M.D. (2005) "Still Doomed to Deficits: An Update on US Trade Elasticities," University of Wisconsin, Madison Working Paper. Available online at: <http://www.ssc.wisc.edu/~mchinn/updated_tradebalance.pdf> (accessed February 28, 2004).

Coates, J.M. and Herbert, J. (2008) "Endogenous Steroids and Financial Risk Taking on a London Trading Floor," *Proceedings of the National Academy of Sciences of the United States of America*, 105(16): 6167–72.

Copeland, L. (2005) *Exchange Rates and International Finance*, Prentice Hall.

Cornford, A. (1996) "Some Recent Innovations in International Finance: Different Faces of Risk Management and Control," *Journal of Economic Issues*, 30(2): 483–508.

Cross, S.Y. (1998) *The Foreign Exchange Market in the United States*, New York: Federal Reserve Bank of New York. Available online at: <http://www.ny.frb.org/pihome/addpub/usfxm/> (accessed 15 November, 2002).

Cruz, M., Amann, E., and Walters, B. (2006) "Expectations, the Business Cycle, and the Mexican Peso Crisis," *Cambridge Journal of Economics*, 30: 701–22.

Cumby, R. (1988) "Is it Risk? Explaining Deviations from Uncovered Interest Parity," *Journal of Monetary Economics*, 22(2): 279–99.

Cypher, J.M. (1996) "Mexico: Financial Fragility or Structural Crisis?" *Journal of Economic Issues*, 30(2): 451–61.

Davidson, P. (1982–83) "Rational Expectations: A Fallacious Foundation for Studying Crucial Decision-Making Processes," *Journal of Post Keynesian Economics*, 5(2): 182–98.

Davidson, P. (1992–93) "Reforming the World's Money," *Journal of Post Keynesian Economics*, 15(2): 153–79.

Davidson, P. (1994) *Post Keynesian Macroeconomic Theory: A Foundation for Successful Economic Policies for the Twenty-first Century*, Aldershot, UK: Edward Elgar.

Davidson, P. (1997) "Are Grains of Sand in the Wheels of International Finance Sufficient to Do the Job When *Boulders* Are Often Required?" *Economic Journal*, 107(442): 671–86.

Davidson, P. (1999) "Global Employment and Open Economy Macroeconomics," in J. Deprez and J.T. Harvey (eds), *Foundations of International Economics: Post Keynesian Perspectives*, London: Routledge: 9–34.

Davidson, P. (2002) "Globalization," *Journal of Post Keynesian Economics*, 24(3): 475–492.

Davidson, P. (2003) "Are Fixed Exchange Rates the Problem and Flexible Exchange Rates the Cure?" *Eastern Economics Journal*, 29(2): 259–68.

Davidson, P. (2006) "The Declining Dollar, Global Economic Growth, and Macro Stability," *Journal of Post Keynesian Economics*, 28(3): 473–93.

Davidson, P. and Smolensky, E. (1964) *Aggregate Supply and Demand Analysis*, New York: Harper and Row, Publishers.

Dornbusch, R. (1976) "Expectations and Exchange Rate Dynamics," *Journal of Political Economy*, 84(6):1161–76.

Economic Report of the President (2006) *2006 Economic Report of the President*, Washington, D.C.: United States Government Printing Office.

Eichengreen, B., Tobin, J., and Wyplosz, C. (1995) "The Case for Sand in the Wheels of International Finance," *Economic Journal*, 105 (428): 162–72.

Evans, M.D.D. and Lyons, R.K. (2002) "Order Flow and Exchange Rate Dynamics," *Journal of Political Economy*, 110(1): 170–80.

Fatum, R. (2000) "On the Effectiveness of Sterilized Foreign Exchange Intervention," Santa Cruz Center for International Economics Working Paper #99-2. Available online at: <http://sccie.ucsc.edu/papers/workingpapers/99/sccie-99-2.pdf> (accessed 15 November, 2002).

Feeny, M. and Brooks, J. (1991) "The Dealing Room and the Dealer," in R. Weisweiller (ed.), *Managing a Foreign Exchange Department: A Manual of Effective Practice*, 2nd edn, New York: Quorum Books:17–33.

Flood, M.D. (1994) "Market Structure and Inefficiency in the Foreign Exchange Market," *Journal of International Money and Finance*, 13(2): 131–58.

Frankel, J., Galli, G., and Giovannini, A. (1996) *The Microstructure of Foreign Exchange Markets*, Chicago: The University of Chicago Press.

Frankel, J.A. and Froot, K.A. (1986) "Understanding the US Dollar in the Eighties: The Expectations of Chartists and Fundamentalists," *The Economic Record*, supplement: 24–38.

Grabel, I. (1996) "Stock Markets, Rentier Interest, and the Current Mexican Crisis," *Journal of Economic Issues*, 30(2): 443–9.

Grabel, I. (1999) "Emerging Stock Markets and Third World Development: The Post Keynesian Case for Pessimism," in J. Deprez and J.T. Harvey (eds), *Foundations of International Economics: Post Keynesian Perspectives*, London: Routledge: 229–47.

Grabel, I. (2003) "Averting Crisis? Assessing Measures to Manage Financial Integration in Emerging Economies," *Cambridge Journal of Economics*, 27(3): 317–36.

Gradojevic, N. and Neeley, C.J. (2008) "The Dynamic Interaction of Order Flows and the CAD/USD Exchange Rate," Federal Reserve Bank of St. Louis, Working Papers: 2008-006. Available online at: <http://research.stlouisfed.org/wp/2008/2008-006.pdf> (accessed 2 May, 2008).

Harvey, J.T. (1993a) "Daily Exchange Rate Variance," *Journal of Post Keynesian Economics*, 15(4): 515–40.

Harvey, J.T. (1993b) "The Institution of Foreign Exchange Trading," *Journal of Economic Issues*, 27(3): 679–98.

Harvey, J.T. (1996a) "Long-term Exchange Rate Movements: The Role of the Fundamentals in Neoclassical Models of Exchange Rates," *Journal of Economic Issues*, 30(2): 509–16.

Harvey, J.T. (1996b) "Orthodox Approaches to Exchange Rate Determination: A Survey," *Journal of Post Keynesian Economics*, 18(4): 567–83.

Harvey, J.T. (1998) "Heuristic Judgment Theory," *Journal of Economic Issues*, 32(1): 47–64.

Harvey, J.T. (1998–99) "The Nature of Expectations in the Foreign Exchange Market: A Test of Competing Theories," *Journal of Post Keynesian Economics*, 21(2): 181–200.

Harvey, J.T. (2001) "Exchange Rate Theory and 'The Fundamentals,'" *Journal of Post Keynesian Economics*, 24(1): 3–15.

Harvey, J.T. (2002a) "Determinants of Currency Market Forecasts: An Empirical Study," *Journal of Post Keynesian Economics*, 25(1): 33–49.

Harvey, J.T. (2002b) "Keynes' Chapter Twenty-Two: A System Dynamics Model," *Journal of Economic Issues*, 26(2): 373–82.

Harvey, J.T. (2004) "Deviations from Uncovered Interest Rate Parity: A Post Keynesian Explanation," *Journal of Post Keynesian Economics*, 27(1): 19–35.

Harvey, J.T. (2006a) "Modeling Interest Rate Parity: A System Dynamics Approach," *Journal of Economic Issues*, 40(2): 395–403.

Harvey, J.T. (2006b) "Psychological and Institutional Forces and the Determination of Exchange Rates," *Journal of Economic Issues* (40)1: 153–70.

Harvey, J.T. and Quinn, S. (1997) "Expectations and Rational Expectations in the Foreign Exchange Market," *Journal of Economic Issues*, 31(2): 615–22.

Heiner, R. (1983) "The Origin of Predictable Behavior," *American Economic Review*, 73(4): 560–95.

Hudson, N.R.L. (1979) *Money and Exchange Dealing in International Banking*, New York: John Wiley and Sons.

International Monetary Fund (2002) *International Financial Statistics: Data CD*, September, Washington, DC: International Monetary Fund.

Ito, T. (1990) "Foreign Exchange Rate Expectations: Micro Survey Data,"*American Economic Review*, 80(3): 434–49.

Jackson, K.D. (1999) "Introduction: The Roots of the Crisis," in K.D. Jackson (ed.), *Asian Contagion: The Causes and Consequences of a Financial Crisis*, Boulder, CO: Westview Press, 1–27.

Keller, R.R. and Carlson, J.L. (1982) "A Neglected Chapter in Keynes' General Theory." *Journal of Post Keynesian Economics*, 4(3): 404–12.

Keynes, J.M. (1964) *The General Theory of Employment, Interest, and Money*, San Diego: Harcourt Brace Jovanovich.

Keynes, J.M. (1980) *The Collected Writings of John Maynard Keynes: Volume 25*, D. Moggridge (ed.), London: Macmillan.

Kindleberger, C.P. (2000) *Manias, Panics, and Crashes: A History of Financial Crises*, 4th edn, New York: Wiley.

Krause, L.A. (1991) *Speculation and the Dollar: The Political Economy of Exchange Rates*, Boulder, Colorado: Westview Press.

Kregel, J. (2004) "Can We Create a Stable International Financial Environment that Ensures net Resource Transfers to Developing Countries?" *Journal of Post Keynesian Economics*, 26(4): 573–90.

Lauridsen, L.S. (1998) "Thailand: Causes, Conduct, Consequences," in K.S. Jomo (ed.) *Tigers in Trouble: Financial Governance, Liberalisation and Crises in East Asia*, London: Zed Books: 137–61.

Lavoie, M. (2000) "A Post Keynesian View of Interest Parity Theorems," *Journal of Post Keynesian Economics*, 23(1): 163–79.

Lavoie, M. (2001) "The Reflux Mechanism and the Open Economy," in L.P. Rochon and M. Vernengo (eds), *Credit, Interest Rates and the Open Economy: Essays on Horizontalism*, Cheltenham, UK: Edward Elgar: 215–42.

Lavoie, M. (2002–03) "Interest Parity, Risk Premia, and Post Keynesian Analysis," *Journal of Post Keynesian Economics*, 25(2): 237–49.

Lim, J. (2004) "Macroeconomic Implications of the Southeast Asian Crises," in K.S. Jomo (ed.) *After the Storm: Crisis, Recovery and Sustaining Development in Four Asian Economies*, Singapore: Singapore University Press: 40–74.

Lopez, J. (1998) "External Financial Fragility and Capital Flight in Mexico," *International Review of Applied Economics*, 12(2): 257–70.

Lopez-Gallardo, J., Moreno-Brid, J.C., and Anyul, M.P. (2006) "Financial Fragility and Financial Crisis in Mexico," *Metroeconomica*, 57(3): 365–88.

MacDonald, R. (1995) "Long-Run Exchange Rate Modeling: A Survey of the Recent Evidence," *IMF Staff Papers*, 42(3): 437–89.

MacDonald, R. and Taylor, M.P. (1992) "Exchange Rate Economics: A Survey," *IMF Staff Papers*, 39(1): 1–57.

Margolis, L. (1990) "Before and After October 19: Structural Changes in U.S. Financial Markets," in D.R. Siegle (ed.), *Innovation and Technology in the Markets: A Reordering of the World's Capital Market Systems*, Chicago: Probus Publishing Company: 59–70.

McCombie, J.S.L. (2003) "Balance-of-Payments-Constrained Economic Growth," in J.E. King (ed.) *The Elgar Companion to Post Keynesian Economics*, Cheltenham, UK: Edward Elgar: 15–20.

Meese, R. and Rogoff, K. (1983) "Empirical Exchange Rate Models of the 1970s: Do They Fit Out of Sample?" *Journal of International Economics*, 14(1–2): 3–24.

Minsky, H.P. (1982) *Can "It" Happen Again?* Armonk, NY: M.E. Sharpe.

Minsky, H.P. (1992) "The Financial Instability Hypothesis," The Jerome Levy Economics Institute Working Paper Number 74. Available online at: <http://www.levy.org/pubs/wp74.pdf> (accessed October 22, 2007).

Minsky, H.P. (1996) *Stabilizing an Unstable Economy*, New Haven: Yale University Press.

Moosa, I.A. (2002) "A Test of the Post Keynesian Hypothesis on Expectation Formation in the Foreign Exchange Market," *Journal of Post Keynesian Economics*, 24(3): 443–57.

Moosa, I.A. (2004) "An Empirical Examination of the Post Keynesian View of Forward Exchange Rates," *Journal of Post Keynesian Economics*, 26(3): 395–418.

Moosa, I.A. (2007–08) "Neoclassical versus Post Keynesian Models of Exchange Rate Determination: A Comparison Based on Nonnested Model Selection Tests and Predictive Accuracy," *Journal of Post Keynesian Economics*, 30(2): 169–85.

Neeley, C.J. (1999) "An Introduction to Capital Controls," *Federal Reserve Bank of St. Louis Review*, November/December: 13–30.

Oberlechner, T. (2004) *The Psychology of the Foreign Exchange Market*, Chichester, UK: John Wiley and Sons.

Petridis, R. (1999) "Neoclassical Economics," in P.A. O'Hara (ed.) *Encyclopedia of Political Economy*, London: Routledge: 788–93.

Pilbeam, K. (1994) "Chartists, Fundamentalists, and Simpletons: An Evaluation of Alternative Exchange Rate Trading Strategies," *British Review of Economic Issues*, 16(39): 65–83.

Pilbeam, K. (2005) *International Finance*, Palgrave MacMilllan.

Phongpaichit, P. and Baker, C. (2004) "Aftermath: Structural Change and Policy Innovation after the Thai Crisis," in K.S. Jomo (ed.) *After the Storm: Crisis, Recovery and Sustaining Development in Four Asian Economies*, Singapore: Singapore University Press: 150–72.

Quinn, S.F. and Harvey, J.T. (1998) "Speculation and the Dollar in the 1980s," *Journal of Economic Issues*, 32(2): 315–23.

Rapach, D.E. and Wohar, M.E. (2002) "Testing the Monetary Model of Exchange Rate Determination: New Evidence from a Century of Data," *Journal of International Economics*, 58(2): 359–85.

Redelmeier, D.A. and Tversky, A. (1992) "On the Framing of Multiple Prospects," *Psychological Science*, 3(3): 191–3.

Rogoff, Kenneth. (1996) "The Purchasing Power Parity Puzzle," *Journal of Economic Literature*, 34(2): 647–68.

Rogoff, Kenneth. (2001) "The Failure of Empirical Exchange Rate Models: No Longer New but Still True," *Economic Policy Web Essay*, 1(1). Available online at: http://www.economic-policy.org/pdfs/Kenneth%20Rogoffwebsa.pdf (accessed June 22, 2006).

Rogoff, Kenneth. (2002) "Dornbusch's Overshooting Model After Twenty-Five Years," *International Monetary Fund Staff Papers*, 49: 1–34.

Rosenberg, M. (1987) "Traders Make Tradeoffs," *American Banker*, July 30: 33.

Rosenberg, M.R. (1996) *Currency Forecasting: A Guide to Fundamental and Technical Models of Exchange Rate Determination*, Chicago: Irwin.

Salvatore, D. (2004) *International Economics*, John Wiley and Sons, Inc.

Sarno, L. and Taylor, M.P. (2002) "Purchasing Power Parity and the Real Exchange Rate," *International Monetary Fund Staff Papers*, 49(1): 65–105.

Schulmeister, S. (1987) *An Essay on Exchange Rate Dynamics*, Research Unit Labour Market and Employment Discussion Paper 87-8, Berlin: Wissenschaftzentrum Berlin für Sozialforschung.

Schulmeister, S. (1988) "Currency Speculation and Dollar Fluctuations," *Banca Nazionale Del Lavoro Quarterly Review*, December: 343–65.

Schwager, J.D. (1992) *The New Market Wizards: Conversations with America's Top Traders*, New York: Harper Collins.

Schwartz, H. (1998) *Rationality Gone Awry? Decision Making Inconsistent with Economic and Financial Theory*, Westport, Connecticut: Praeger.

Scott, R.E. (2006) "Trade Picture," The Economic Policy Institute report, February 10, 2006. Available online at: <http://www.epinet.org/content.cfm/webfeatures_econindicators_tradepict20060210> (accessed September 9, 2007).

Shaikh, A. (1980) "The Law of International Exchange," in E.J. Nell (ed.), *Growth, Profits, and Property*, Cambridge: Cambridge University Press.

Shaikh, A. (1996) "Free Trade, Unemployment, and Economic Policy," in J. Eatwell (ed.) *Global Unemployment: Loss of Jobs in the 90's*, Armonk, New York: M.E. Sharpe.

Shaikh, A. and Antonopoulos, R. (1998) "Explaining Long Term Exchange Rate Behavior in the United States and Japan," The Jerome Levy Economics Institute Working Paper Number 250. Available online at: <http://www.levy.org/default.asp?view=publications_view&pubID=f73a204a73> (accessed June 25, 2006).

Shelton, J. (1994) *Money Meltdown: Restoring order to the Global Currency System*, New York: The Free Press.

Sheng, Y.K. and Kirinpanu, S. (2000) "Once Only the Sky was the Limit: Bangkok's Housing Boom and the Financial Crisis in Thailand." *Housing Studies*, 15(1): 11–27.

Shoup, G. (1998) *The International Guide to Foreign Currency Management*, Chicago: Glenlake Publishing Company, Ltd.

Smithin, J. (1999) "Money and National Sovereignty in the Global Economy." *Eastern Economic Journal*, 25(1): 49–61.

Smithin, J. (2002–03) "Interest Parity, Purchasing Power Parity, "Risk Premia," and Post Keynesian Economic Analysis." *Journal of Post Keynesian Economics*, 25(2): 219–35.

Suvanto, A. (1993) *Foreign Exchange Dealing: Essays on the Microstructure of the Foreign Exchange Market*, Helsinki: The Research Institute of the Finnish Economy.

Taylor, M.P. (1987) "Covered Interest Parity: A High-Frequency, High-Quality Data Study," *Economica*, 54 (216): 429–38.

Taylor, M.P. (1995a) "The Economics of Exchange Rates," *Journal of Economic Literature*, 33(1): 13–47.

Taylor, M.P. (1995b) "Exchange Rate Modelling and Macro Fundamentals: Failed Partnership or Open Marriage?" *British Review of Economic Issues*, 17(42): 1–41.

Taylor, M.P. and Allen, H. (1992) "The Use of Technical Analysis in the Foreign Exchange Market," *Journal of International Money and Finance*, 11(3): 304–14.

Tobin, J. (1978) "A Proposal for International Monetary Reform," *Eastern Economic Journal*, 4: 153–59.

Tversky, A. and Kahneman, D. (1974) "Judgment under Uncertainty: Heurisitics and Biases," *Science*, 185: 1124–31.

Taylor, M.P. (1988) "Rational Choice and the Framing of Decisions," in D.E. Bell, H. Raiffa, and A. Tversky (eds), *Decision Making: Descriptive, Normative, and Prescriptive Interactions*, Cambridge: Cambridge University Press: 167–92.

Taylor, M.P. (1992) "Advances in Prospect Theory: Cumulative Representation of Uncertainty," *Journal of Risk and Uncertainty* 5: 297–323.

Tversky, A. and Koehler, D.J. (1994) "Support Theory: A Nonextensional Representation of Subjective Probability," *Psychological Review*, 101(4): 547–67.

UNCTAD (2002) *Statistics in Brief*, New York: United Nations Conference on Trade and Development. Available online at: <http://www.unctad.org/Templates/WebFlyer. asp?intItemID=2111&lang=1> (accessed 15 November, 2002).

Visser, H. (2006) *A Guide to International Monetary Economics: Exchange Rate Theories, Systems And Policies*, Aldershot, UK: Edward Elgar.

Walter, A. (1991) *World Power and World Money: Restoring Order to the Global Currency System*, New York: St. Martin's Press.

Weisweiller, R. (ed.) (1991) *Managing a Foreign Exchange Department: A Manual of Effective Practice*, 2nd edn, New York: Quorum Books.

Wolfson, M.H. (2002) "Minsky's Theory of Financial Crisis in a Global Context," *Journal of Economic Issues*, 36(2): 393–400.

World Trade Organization (2005) *International Trade Statistics 2005*, Geneva, Switzerland: World Trade Organization.

Wu, S. (2007) "Interest Rate Risk and the Forward Premium Anomaly in Foreign Exchange Markets," *Journal of Money, Credit, and Banking*, 39(2–3): 423–42.

Index

Printed in the United States
by Baker & Taylor Publisher Services